LIFE
AFTER
PROGRESS

Technology, Community,
and the New Economy

LOCAL FUTURES

Local Futures is an international non-profit organization dedicated to renewing ecological and social well-being by strengthening communities and local economies worldwide.

Published by Local Futures
USA, UK, Australia, Mexico
www.localfutures.org

Design: Cathy Martin
Cover design: Kamya O'Keeffe
Cover photo: Justinian Calugarescu

ISBN 978-1-7329804-1-9

Printed in the United States of America
10 9 8 7 6 5 4 3 2 1

CONTENTS

CONTRIBUTORS

BAYO AKOMOLAFE

HENRY COLEMAN

KUNZANG DEACHEN

STEVEN GORELICK

MARJANA KOS

ALEX JENSEN

ANJA LYNGBAEK

HELENA NORBERG-HODGE

CHOZIN PALMO

JIGMET SINGGE

KRISTEN STEELE

FOREWORD
Bayo Akomolafe, Ph.D.

When Kyah was two, he wandered too close to his aunt's flatscreen television. We aren't quite sure about the sequence of events that unfolded between said wandering and the bone-curdling crash that dragged us all to the living room, to the scene of the crime, silently surveying the bits and pieces of high-definition clarity entangled with the befuddling curls of the rug. All we know, all we remember, is that *it happened*—and that our playful prophet finally made good on his weeks-old toddling threats to upstage the natural order of things.

A day later, we drove to a large warehouse-like place somewhere in Richmond, Virginia. I cannot recall what the place was called, but it would have made Walter Benjamin cry. There were televisions and television accessories everywhere. A circus of screens and grinning pixelated faces. Some TVs were in carton boxes stacked high in an economic hierarchy of means and dollars. They were the more expensive ones. We let our eyes drift away from their advertised promises of unrivaled depth and investigated other aisles-praying that a heavenly gift-bearing stork had already arrived with a replacement we could tuck into our budget. Down the aisle, the other television sets were turned on and lined up, dutifully haranguing the eager consumers with embellished tales of what they could do. They had categories of resolution quality stamped on their corners: HD, Full HD, 4K UHD, 8K UHD. My sister-in-law, intoxicated, edged further and further down the spectrum.

For a moment, when my eyes weren't anxiously surveilling the antics of our waltzing wizard, I wondered about the promise of clarity, the urge towards higher definition, the fascination with precision. What captivatingly lucid television screen stood knighted at the end of the aisle, at the conclusion of my sister-in-law's starry-eyed quest for the very best? *How much clarity* did we really need to have an appreciable experience of, say, George Clooney convincing Matt Damon to join his band of debonair thieves in *Ocean's Eleven*? Was there such a thing as too much clarity? Too much HD? What did clarity leave out?

These questions about clarity visited me again rather forcefully as I thumbed through the publicly released images NASA's newly deployed James Webb Space Telescope had produced of distant galaxies, swirling gas clouds, and alien planets. With every new image published, with every new headline and clickbait title surrounding the Telescope's phallic advances into the dark void, commentators have praised the extraordinary clarity afforded us by the genius of modern science.

Almost as eventful as this technological gift of cosmic clarity are whispers of confusion about our conventional renderings of the beginnings of the universe and its unthinkably vast eras of galactic evolution. There are now papers, YouTube videos, and essays breathlessly proclaiming the new crisis at the heart of astrophysics, the death of the Big Bang theory. Of course, the priests and keepers of the status quo insist nothing has changed. Nothing much. It'll take more than a splodge, a blip or two to dislodge a paradigm.

Being a generalist of sorts, I am not as committed to finding a resolution to the origin of the stars as I am dedicated to sitting with the troubling transversality that hijacks every steady line of progress-so-called, disrupting the details, stirring the waters, and muddling the books like a stowaway divine trickster aboard a transatlantic slave ship. At least at the time of writing, it seems that the more we look, the less we see confirmation of what we thought we knew about stuff. What we were once clear about. The conversations are still ongoing, but somewhere down the line, somewhere along the way to penetrating transparency, the cosmos apparently kicked back, refused subservience to the family business, exercised its right to opacity, and playfully danced away from full view—shattering the screen of our confidence. Breaking the natural order of things.

It's probably clear by now that this book is about clarity. In a way. It is about beginnings. About endings. About progress and what happens in the wake of its loss. About what clarity obscures. *Especially* that. What clarity hides away from view.

This clarity I write of is not just the quality of intelligibility an image might 'have', but the deeply political world-making paradigm of industrial modernity that presumes humans might by and by come to know the world by stabilizing it, by shushing it beneath concrete and steel, and lining it up in a plantation of anthropocentric production. This clarity, a kind of civilizational gentrification, obscures our connections to ecology, our dependence on soil and earthworm and bird and rock and technology. It bends spacetime into a straight line, forcing myriad bodily temporalities to adhere to the rule of homogenous clock time. This clarity hides away the scandalous realization that we are not lords of the realm, and that we do not merely use the world but are used by the world in return.

This 'clarity' is progress. A sensorial monoculture. Sylvia Wynter's colonial 'Man'. Giorgio Agamben's 'Anthropos'. Walter Benjamin's 'phantasmagoria'. Erin Manning's 'clearing'.

Through the stories and essays in this collection, you will discern a single urgent note, a leitmotif for life at the end of progress, a story that the authors of this rich book want to tell you: we live with/in a 'clearing' of sorts—a modern epistemic placemaking ritual that depends on *management*, toxic distances of food production, atomic notions of identity, forward-facing temporalities, philosophies about educational excellence that are predicated upon being divorced from the immediate and the local, and Enlightenment ideas about human separation and separability. *We do not have to live this way.* What passes as natural is a social production that elides other modes of knowing and being known by the world we seek to tame.

You might not think it so—but a ten-billion-dollar telescope purring its way through space and the moment a teenager in Chennai decides to jump in front of a moving train for having been branded a failure by her school are entangled productions of the 'clearing'. And now, perhaps more than ever, the colonial edifice of space-penetrating, ocean-traversing, land-extracting, and world-eliding performances that has sponsored this clearing, buckles under the weight of its own aspirations. In short, when an image spills into its caricature, the dizzying complexity of the subterranean worlds that have held it aloft for so long, new imperatives for living well emerge.

Helena Norberg-Hodge was in the *living room* long before many of us arrived to investigate the crash of things. I remember watching her on my old laptop masterfully convene eloquent critiques of the "inhuman systems" that masqueraded as life itself. Something about the stories she told of the Ladakhi people, the way she articulated the imperatives and promises of 'localization', the way she traced out the sickening rise of giant corporate agencies and their desires to terraform the planet to produce profit even when it meant poisoning communities, helped me connect the dots of my world into a meaningful constellation that still guides my work today as a trans-public intellectual, recovering psychotherapist, and decolonial thought leader. On the weary, low-definition screens of my young academic life, Helena—along with the brilliant folk at Local Futures, some of whom you will meet on the pages of this book—insisted that there were other spaces of power. Manifold elsewheres shrouded by the neon-lit fetishes of modern life.

I recall sensing she was well and truly lost—but only in the wondrous way that is suggested when my people, the Yoruba of West Africa, say "to find your way, you must become lost. Generously so."

This book is a cartography of sensations guiding us through the din of demise. A map to shake you out of the complacency of being so thoroughly found, so thoroughly intelligible, so worryingly available to the imaginations of the familiar.

There are worlds in the wilds beyond our fences. To see them, the paradigms and geometries of clarity would have to be toppled, composted into the befuddling curls of ecology. There, on the ground, we will have brilliant new visions – ones that the very latest television screens cannot picture.

INTRODUCTION
Helena Norberg-Hodge and Steven Gorelick

F ar from the old institutions of political power, a people's movement is rising up. All around the world, small-scale initiatives are rebuilding local communities, protecting local ecosystems, and creating resilient local economies. These are all part of a broader movement toward economic localization—the most effective and common sense approach to reversing the damage caused by the corporate-dominated global economy.

For the last four decades, Local Futures—a small organization with a global reach and an important message—has been raising the alarm about the disturbing impacts of economic globalization, while promoting the vision of hope offered by economic localization. The essays in this book—all written by Local Futures staff—are grounded in that vision.

The costs of globalization are immense. By enabling a massive expansion in the scale and power of big business and banking, globalization has created or worsened nearly every problem we face: fundamentalism and ethnic conflict; climate chaos and species extinction; financial instability and unemployment; the erosion of democracy and the rise of authoritarianism. *Life After Progress* touches on all of these, and more.

But the essays that follow are neither pessimistic nor fatalistic, because they also point to economic localization as a strategic way to address our problems simultaneously. The essence of localization involves shortening the distance between producers and consumers, thereby scaling down the power of big business and bringing decision-making back to the regional and local levels. Localization provides the necessary foundation for strong communities, and ultimately leads to a smaller gap between rich and poor. It inherently means reducing unnecessary transport and ending wasteful, carbon-intensive practices that are deemed "efficient" in the global economy, such as shipping fish from Norway to China for de-boning, apples from Europe to South Africa for washing, or shrimp from the UK to Thailand for peeling.

Although written over an extended period of time, the essays that follow remain highly relevant: they are both prescient about the world we live in today, and light a path towards a happier, healthier future for our children and grandchildren.

Life After Progress is an example of the work Local Futures has done throughout its long history. Our roots are in Ladakh, or "Little Tibet", a region in the Indian Himalayas where we have been active since 1978. Our work there aims to strengthen Ladakh's self-reliant traditional culture, while enabling visitors to the region to gain a better understanding of the impacts of globalized development, including mass tourism. We also convene an annual World Localization Day event that celebrates and disseminates information about the thousands of groups and individuals around the world working to strengthen and protect their local economies, communities and environments. Our Economics of Happiness program includes a long-running series of international conferences and an award-winning film of the same name. The film, which lays out a critique of globalization and illustrates the many benefits of localization, has been screened in more than twenty countries at over 1,500 community-organized events. Our Global to Local program focuses on awareness-raising, and includes our many books, videos, reports, blogs, podcasts, webinars and much more. We also produced an online Localization Action Guide, with nearly 150 ideas for local initiatives in food, farming, finance, business, and more. And we are the organizers of the International Alliance for Localization (IAL), a cross-cultural network of individuals and organizations dedicated to protecting and renewing the rich cultural and ecological diversity of the planet.

Life After Progress is a continuation of this long tradition of "education as activism". We not only hope that you find it thought-provoking, but that it spurs you towards concrete action.

1

BEGINNINGS

BELONGING
Helena Norberg-Hodge

I was living in Paris in 1975, when I was asked to go out as part of a film team to Ladakh, or "Little Tibet". In my work as a linguist I had traveled to many parts of the world, including Africa, North and South America, and all over Europe. Nothing had prepared me for what I encountered in Ladakh. High up on the Tibetan plateau, I came to know a people who had never been colonized and were still living according to their own values and principles. Despite a harsh and barren environment of extreme temperatures, the Ladakhis were prospering materially, but also, and even more importantly, emotionally. Over time, I came to realize that they were among the freest, most peaceful and joyous people I had ever met. I also discovered that their happiness translated into a remarkable tolerance, an acceptance of difference and of adversity.

Belonging to Place

When I first arrived, Ladakh was a culture that seemed completely attuned to the needs of people and the environment. An important factor in the environmental balance was undoubtedly the fact that the Ladakhis belonged to their place on earth. They were bonded to that place through intimate daily contact, through knowledge about their immediate surroundings—its changing seasons, needs and limitations. For them, "the environment" was not some alien, problematic sphere of human concern; it was where they lived. They were keenly aware of the living context in which they found themselves. The movement of the stars, the sun, and moon were familiar rhythms that influenced their daily activities. Life rooted in the natural world created a sense of kinship with plants and animals that nurtured a profound respect for the humble creatures that shared the Ladakhis' world. Children and adults who witnessed the birth, rearing, mating and death of the animals around them were unable to view those animals as merely a "natural resource" to be plundered.

For the Ladakhis, there was no need to "manage" their resources; they themselves were a part of the natural balance, and, out of this belonging came the knowledge that enabled them to survive and prosper in such a harsh setting. For example, virtually all the plants, shrubs, and bushes that grew wild, either around the edges of irrigated land or in the mountains—what we would call "weeds"—were gathered and served some useful purpose. *Burtse* was used for fuel and animal fodder; *yagdzas*, for the roofs of houses; the thorny *tsermang*, for building fences to keep animals out of fields and gardens; *demok*, as a red dye. Others were used for medicine, food, incense, and basket weaving. The soil in the stables was dug up to be used as fertilizer, thus recycling animal urine. Dung was collected not only from the stables and pens, but also from the pastures. Even human night soil was not wasted. Each house had composting latrines consisting of a small room with a hole in the floor built above a vertical chute, usually one floor high. Earth and ash from the kitchen stove were added, thus aiding chemical decomposition, producing better fertilizer, and eliminating smells. Once a year the latrine was emptied at ground level and the contents used on the fields. In such ways Ladakhis traditionally recycled everything. There was literally no waste. With only scarce resources at their disposal, the Ladakhis managed to attain almost complete self-reliance, dependent on the outside world only for salt, tea, and a few metals for cooking utensils and tools.

Yet they enjoyed more than mere subsistence. Through adapting their activities to the exigencies of their natural environment and the rhythm of the seasons, the Ladakhis had a remarkably high standard of living. No one was poor; no one went hungry. Although they spent a long time accomplishing each task, they worked at a gentle pace and had a surprising amount of leisure. The traditional way of life was based upon and continually fostered a deep connection with place, which in turn supported community. Ladakhis were thus raised in an enveloping network of extended family, friends, plants and animals.

Belonging to Community

I became close friends with a young Ladakhi woman named Dolma, who had just given birth to her first child. Spending time with her family,

I saw something of how children were brought up. Dolma spent more time with little Angchuk, who was six months old, than anyone else did. But caring for the baby was not her job alone. Everyone looked after him. Someone was always there to kiss and cuddle him. Men and women alike adored little children, and even the teenage boys from next door were not embarrassed to be seen cooing over little Angchuk or rocking him to sleep with a lullaby. Taking responsibility for other children as one grows up has a profound effect on a child's development. For boys in particular, it is important since it brings out their ability for caring and nurturing. In traditional Ladakh, masculine identity was not threatened by such qualities; on the contrary, it embraced them.

Children were never segregated into peer groups; they grew up surrounded by people of all ages, from young babies to great-grandparents. With the exception of religious training in the monasteries, the traditional culture had no separate process called "education". Instead it was the product of an intimate relationship with the community and its environment. Children learned from grandparents, family, and friends. They learned about connections, process, and change, about the intricate web of fluctuating relationships in the natural world around them. When villagers gathered to discuss important issues, or had festivals and parties, children of all ages were always present. Even at social gatherings that ran late into the night with drinking, singing, dancing, and loud music, young children could be seen running around, joining in the festivities until they simply dropped off to sleep. In the West, we would say the children were being "spoiled" by their freedom, but in fact very soon, by the time they were five or so, Ladakhi children learned to take responsibility for someone else, carrying infants on their backs when they were strong enough.

Old people also participated in all spheres of life, from working to childcare. For the elderly in Ladakh, there were no years of staring into space, unwanted and alone; they were important members of the community until the day they died. Old age implied years of valuable experience and wisdom. Grandparents were not so strong, but they had other qualities to contribute; there was no hurry to life, so if they worked more slowly it did not matter. One of the main reasons old people remained so alive and involved was their constant contact with the young. The relationship between grandparent and child was different from that between parent and child. The very oldest and the very youngest formed a special bond; they were often best friends.

Comparing what I have just described with the experience of growing up and aging in the West, the differences are obvious. And our children are bearing the brunt of it. From the technology and pharmaceutical-based hospital birth to the crowded day care center, from the Ritalin prescriptions to the television babysitter, from standardized, segregated education to video games—growing up in the West is a world away from what I saw in Ladakh. We cannot lay the blame on Western parents; for they too are victims of the global economy and, in most cases, are doing the best they can.

Through economic and societal forces we have been segregated into smaller and smaller social units. Those who are not fortunate enough to be part of a nuclear family are often isolated and alone. This is most apparent during holidays—Christmas, Thanksgiving, Valentine's Day—but it is actually the case every day of the year. Being single is usually a much more lonely experience in the industrialized world than in a culture where the community is like a close-knit extended family. My husband and I have no children and we feel a much greater sense of loss when we are in the West than we do in Ladakh. There, we are integrated into the larger community and become part of a wider network of caregivers for the children.

Living Harmoniously

Having lived in many different cultures, I have become convinced that we are shaped by culture to a far greater extent than we realize—an influence that extends throughout our entire lives. My husband and I would regularly spend many months in Ladakh without having a single argument. But within hours of leaving Ladakh, finding ourselves in New Delhi or London, tensions built up enough to cause friction between us. In Ladakh, we lived in a human-scale community where people were seen and heard and recognized as individuals, and were deeply connected to the people around us. We not only belonged to a community, we also benefited from daily exercise in the fresh air and in

beautiful surroundings. Our pace of life was based on natural rhythms—
on the rhythms that we, as human beings, have evolved with.

In my daily life in Ladakh, almost everything I needed to have or
to do was within walking distance. Going back and forth to Ladakh, I
have come to value this more and more. In Ladakh, I could walk out of
the house and go uphill for about twenty minutes and be in complete
wilderness. En route, I would have passed some smiling cows and sheep,
maybe a few donkeys, crossed some lively streams and said hello to one
or two people. If I walked twenty minutes downhill from the house, I'd
encounter perhaps a dozen friendly faces along the way before finding
myself in the center of town.

The importance of exercise and fresh air for our wellbeing and for
a sense of belonging to life cannot be overestimated. Modern scientific
research is beginning to back this up: a study in the UK showed that 90
percent of people suffering from depression experienced an increase in
self-esteem after a walk in a park. After a visit to a shopping center, on
the other hand, 44 percent felt a decrease in self-esteem and 22 percent
felt more depressed. [1]

One of the most important factors contributing to a greater sense
of wellbeing is living at a slower pace, with the spaciousness it provides.
In traditional Ladakh, time pressures were non-existent. Even at the
peak of harvest season, everything was done at a leisurely and gracious
pace. There was time for laughter and celebration and constant song.
Humans and animals set the speed, not machines. In the West, we have
come to belong less to life and more to technology. Instead of saving
time, our machine-dependent way of life has left us less and less time
for our families and ourselves.

Learning from Ladakh

I am convinced that it is the need to be loved, rather than innate greed,
that drives us as human beings, driving even our desire for the products
of the consumer culture. People not only need to give and receive love,
they have a great capacity for contentedness, cooperation and generosity.

Yet the globalized consumer culture undermines these qualities at
every turn. Advertising and the media promise people that they will

"belong" and be loved and admired if they wear a certain brand of clothing or have the latest techno-gadget. Children and youth are especially vulnerable to these messages. They hanker after the latest trends in the hopes of gaining the respect and love of their peers. In reality, consuming leads to greater competition, envy, and eventually, separation.

The globalized consumer culture disconnects us from one another and from the natural world. It blinds us to what is essential for happiness and wellbeing. It takes away our sense of belonging—to community, to place, to the earth—and replaces it with feelings of insecurity, inferiority and disconnectedness. This in turn fuels greed and increased consumerism. I'm convinced that most of our crises stem from the breakdown of community and our spiritual connection to the living world.

Recognizing this truth empowers us. Realizing that it's not human nature that is to blame, but rather an inhuman system, is actually inspiring. Looking at the bigger picture in this way is essential to effecting long-lasting change; it can also help us to realize that the same economic policies that are breaking down community are destroying the environment. As more people become aware of this, support is growing— from social as well as environmental movements—for a fundamental shift in direction.

Reweaving the Fabric of Belonging

In order to create the structures that support a sense of belonging we need to rebuild community, and that means rebuilding ways of meeting our needs that allow us to see our impact on others and on the natural world. We need to adapt economic activity to place by shortening the distance between producers and consumers: in other words, we need to localize, rather than globalize, our economies. In this way producers can respond to the needs of consumers, and take responsibility for what they produce as they see the effects immediately before them.

Localization is a process that inherently nurtures a sense of connection to community and to the earth. Strong local economies are essential for helping us to rediscover what it means to belong to a culture, to belong to a community, to belong to a place on earth.

In traditional cultures like Ladakh, spiritual teachings are a constant reminder of belonging: a reminder of our inextricable interdependence with one another and with everything in the cosmos. This reminder is ever present in daily affairs, in rituals and in words of wisdom, passed on from the elders to the young ones.

The story of Ladakh has captured the hearts and minds of countless people, from Mongolia to the USA, from Myanmar to my native country of Sweden. As a consequence, I've been in touch with literally thousands of individuals and projects that are reweaving the fabric of connection, of belonging to place. These movements are rooted in people's desire to preserve the bonds to family, community, and nature that make life meaningful. Taken together, these efforts to reweave the fabric of place-based culture are key elements of an emerging localization movement.

September 10, 2010

TRADITION AND CHANGE
Helena Norberg-Hodge

All around the globe, there is a rising sense that we are entering a time of historic change. Whether this change will be brought on by a destabilizing climate or a chronically collapsing economy, a peaking of oil supplies or intensifying geopolitical tensions, more and more people are concluding that the current system is broken and needs to be replaced.

Awareness is also growing that the same global economic system that threatens the ecological fabric of our world has a profoundly negative impact on our personal lives. The ability of mobile corporations to cut wages, to move jobs elsewhere and to subvert the political process is not only responsible for a widening gap between rich and poor but for increasing psychological breakdown. Depression and addiction are being accelerated by economic processes that erode community while promoting a consumer mindset in which material gain equals happiness.

People want change. But imagining a genuine alternative to the corporate-led global economy is a huge challenge for people who have only known a "modern," industrial way of life—it's like trying to imagine a new color. Viable options are ignored by the media, which instead focuses on market-based pseudo-solutions that attempt to reconcile growth with sustainability. Meanwhile governments, wedded to the belief that a rising GDP will solve all problems, continue to cater to the wishes of large corporations.

We need an enlightened vision that moves beyond the economic growth paradigm. At the same time, we need to abandon the old rhetoric of capitalism vs. communism, and instead address the process that shapes our world today—namely globalization, the continued deregulation of global banks and corporations through trade treaties. This furthers other processes—centralization, urbanization and standardization—that we have been told are inevitable and evolutionary, despite the fact that they are actually driven by policy choices.

For 40 years, my organization, Local Futures, has been promoting a fundamental shift in direction—away from globalizing and towards localizing economic activity. Localization, which shortens the distance between production and consumption, is a "solution multiplier": it dramatically reduces CO2 emissions, energy consumption, and waste; it lays the groundwork for the widespread restoration of cultural and biological diversity; it creates meaningful and secure livelihoods for the entire global population; and, perhaps most importantly of all, it rebuilds the fabric of connection between people, as well as between people and the natural world. It's the economics of happiness.

I had my eyes opened to the key ways in which the economy affects every aspect of our lives while working as a linguist in Ladakh, in the Indian Himalayas, in the mid-1970s. This region was quite unique in that it was completely sealed off until 1974, when it was thrown open to the outside economy. While traditional life in Ladakh was not perfect, the village-based economy was founded on the principles of collaboration and interdependence, which bolstered the connections between people, their community and their local environment. It gave rise to peace, sustainability and the most remarkable *joie de vivre* I had ever experienced.

But over the next decades, I witnessed the social upheaval and environmental destruction brought by conventional development. In Ladakh, I saw how a government-subsidized fossil-fuel based infrastructure for global trade completely undermined the local economy and its livelihoods—for example, by enabling heavily subsidized, chemically preserved butter from the other side of the Himalayas to be sold for half the price of local butter. I saw how, after just a few years, the undermining of the local economy led to unemployment, pulled people into intense competition for scarce jobs in an urban center and ultimately resulted in conflict and violence.

The products that flooded the region created environmental problems that remain unsolved today—from plastic waste and air pollution to pesticides. Even more importantly, the glossy, westernized images of perfection used to advertise these products worked to destabilize the Ladakhi sense of self, leading to heartbreaking psychological and spiritual insecurity. This trend was compounded by the introduction of western-style schooling, which pulled children away from family and community. It replaced the location-specific knowledge that had sustained Ladakhi culture for centuries with a degraded version of an education suitable for an urbanized consumer culture.

In the same way that globalization created unemployment in Ladakh, job security almost everywhere is threatened by "free-trade" treaties that give giant corporations the right to scour the globe in search of the cheapest labor, lowest taxes and weakest environmental standards. Just as glamorous images of westernized perfection eroded the Ladakhis' self-respect, advertisers and marketers in the West continue to drive rampant consumerism by making us feel inadequate if we don't have the latest smartphone or the perfect figure, leading to crippling insecurities. And just as huge subsidies for distantly produced goods rendered local production in Ladakh uneconomic, subsidies provided by nearly every government for fossil fuels and trade-based infrastructures work to the advantage of large, global players at the expense of their smaller, more localized competitors.

For too long, we have been kept blind to this system, distracted by a theater of media-figure scandals and left-right politics that plays with our emotions and obscures the root causes of our social and environmental problems. We have been made to believe that our only means of resistance to the exploitation of both workers and the environment is to buy "ethically produced" or "green" products, thereby allowing ourselves to be reduced from citizens to mere consumers.

I believe that it is mainly blindness that has allowed this destructive system to escalate, and that if enough thinking, caring people are exposed to a big picture global-to-local analysis, single-issue campaigns will unite to form a movement that is strong and diverse enough to challenge the existing political and economic order, and to push for *localization* as a systemic alternative to corporate-led globalization. This is already beginning to happen, as demonstrated by the fight against the TPP (Trans-Pacific Partnership) trade deal: environmentalists, labor unions, small farmers, social justice activists and indigenous rights activists all stood together, united against further corporate deregulation.

Meanwhile, hundreds and thousands of on-the-ground localization initiatives have sprung up around the world. Farmers' markets, transition towns, community gardens, local business alliances, time-banking schemes, alternative schools and many more have proliferated in recent years and are already demonstrating the profound benefits of strengthening local ties. In these places, the fabric of interdependence is being rewoven, and ethnic, racial, socio-economic and intergenerational rifts mended.

One of the most heartening examples of localization in action is the local food movement, which has grown by leaps and bounds in recent decades. Central to the vision is the right of every human being to have fresh, local food at a reasonable price, which means prioritizing local production for local needs over production for export. The economic structure that facilitates this agenda is the local market, which demands of producers a diverse variety of products rather than a massive quantity of a single globally marketed commodity, thereby supporting agricultural and ecological diversity. A diversified farm, in turn, requires less chemicals and less machinery and instead requires the care of human hands, simultaneously reducing reliance on energy and providing many more jobs. Finally, social ties are strengthened on both the production and consumption sides: work on the small, diversified farm is by nature social, and so is shopping at the local market—one study showed that the average shopper at the farmers' market has ten times more conversations than the average shopper at the supermarket. In these ways, localization is the economics of happiness.

Localization is not a guarantee for peace, joy and sustainability, but it is indeed a prerequisite for them. Just as the global economy is rooted in harmful structures that perpetuate blindness, greed and tunnel-vision economics, local economies structurally confer increased visibility of the effects of our actions as consumers as well as citizens and foster closer connections between people and the Earth. There is no blueprint for localization; only the insistence that societies and cultures be allowed to develop according to the dictates of local climate and place, respecting their own priorities, needs and local conditions rather than the profit imperatives of global banks and corporations.

In just the past few years, there has been an international awakening to the need for fundamental change. Sadly, rising dissatisfaction with the status quo has provided opportunities for the emergence of demagogues who speak to our fears and anxieties with the language of xenophobia and scapegoating. This is not the change we want or need, and we must be clear about that with ourselves and with others.

If we wish to build a truly better world, we need to engage in both political resistance and community-level renewal, linking hands with those in our own communities and across the world. We can point to the far-reaching benefits of revitalizing local economies that have already been felt in every corner of the globe. These projects should give all of us reason to hope: if the movement for localization grows fast enough, it will enable us to tackle our global crises before it's too late.

July 5, 2017

WHAT IS THE MEANING OF LIFE?
Helena Norberg-Hodge

Before I went to Ladakh, I would have answered this question very differently. Like many Westerners, I thought meaning was to be found in personal accomplishments. Our fast-paced, competitive, consumer culture molds us into believing that our worth is determined by how we look, the money we make, how much success we have—whether it's as a banker, a teacher or an artist. The emphasis is always on the individual. Advertising and the media convince us that to be worthy, to belong, even to be loved, you need to have the newest gadgets and keep up with the latest fashions.

Fortunately for me, my approach to life changed dramatically after experiencing this ancient Tibetan culture. There I experienced the most joyful people I had ever encountered, and learned that what gives true meaning to life is *connection*—to the natural world and to other human beings.

I have experienced this in many other more traditional communities, which has reinforced my convictions. Despite differences in geography and race, these cultures have this one thing in common: a deep connection to life. This expands outwards from the connections we form with others in our communities and to the living world around us; to the landscape, to the plants, to the animals. When we are deprived of these connections—isolated in a cut-throat, "me-me-me" world, we become not only unhappy, but ill from this deprivation.

Another lesson I learned in Ladakh is that this modern individualistic culture is not an inevitable product of human nature. It is actually our global economic system that severs connections at every turn. Nature has become a commodity and our time is owned by the market. This economy also breeds a kind of thinking that blinds us to what is essential for happiness and wellbeing. It takes away our sense of belonging, to community, place, and the earth, and replaces it with feelings of insecurity, inferiority and disconnectedness. This in turn fuels greed and increased consumerism. Most of our major ecological and social crises—climate change, inequality, terrorism—stem from this breakdown of community and our spiritual connection to the living world.

Over the last few decades, I have seen a heartening countercurrent to the direction the global economy has been taking us. Around the world, countless initiatives have emerged, reweaving the meaningful connections of life. Structurally, these take the form of farmers markets, decentralized renewable energy, local business alliances, outdoor schools, community credit unions and many, many others. They are all part of a growing movement for economic localization.

We can overcome the system that encourages greed and rampant consumerism. This requires both resistance and renewal: resisting the policies of globalization that are socially and environmentally destructive, while renewing the structures that foster connection and genuine sustainability. By rebuilding human-scale communities and local economies around the world—what I call small-scale on a large-scale—we can maintain some of the true benefits of modern society, while reestablishing the connections that give our lives meaning. We can learn from the past and other cultures without going backwards, but instead towards a more humane and meaningful future.

February 11, 2016

2

BREAKDOWN

GLOBALIZATION AND THE AMERICAN DREAM

Helena Norberg-Hodge and Steven Gorelick

"... America is a new kind of society that produces a new kind of human being. That human being—confident, self-reliant, tolerant, generous, future-oriented—is a vast improvement over the wretched, servile, fatalistic and intolerant human being that traditional societies have always produced."
— Dinesh D'Souza, *What's So Great About America*, 2002

Implicit in all the rhetoric promoting globalization is the premise that the rest of the world can and should be brought up to the standard of living of the West, and America in particular. For much of the world the American Dream—though a constantly moving target—is globalization's ultimate endpoint.

But if this is the direction globalization is taking the world, it is worth examining where America itself is headed. A good way to do so is to take a hard look at America's children, since so many features of the global monoculture have been in place their whole lives. If the American Dream isn't working for them, why should anyone anywhere believe it will work for their own children?

As it turns out, children in the US are far from "confident, self-reliant, tolerant, generous, and future-oriented". One indication of this is that more than 7.2 million American children and adolescents require psychiatric drugs; over 2 million are on antidepressants, and another 1.4 million are on anti-anxiety drugs. Drugs are prescribed for shockingly young children; 250,000 children 0-3 years old are taking drugs to combat anxiety. [1]

Most people in the "less developed" world would find it hard to imagine how toddlers could be so anxious that they need psychiatric help. Equally difficult to fathom are many other symptoms of social breakdown among America's children, such as eating disorders. Incidences of anorexia, bulimia and other eating disorders have doubled since the 1960s, and girls are developing these problems at younger and younger ages.[2]

If eating disorders are the bane of America's young girls, violence is a more common problem for its boys. Consider the fact that there have been more than 170 school shootings in the US since 1990, claiming 193 lives. The youngest killer? A six-year-old boy.[3]

Sometimes the violence is directed inward, resulting in suicide. In America today, suicide is the third leading cause of death for 15- to 24-year olds. In 2016, 16 percent of US high school students had seriously considered suicide during the preceding year.[4]

What has made America's children so insecure and troubled? A number of causes are surely involved, most of which can be linked to the global economy. For example, as corporations scour the world for bigger subsidies and lower costs, jobs move with them and families as well. On average, Americans move eleven times during their lives, repeatedly severing connections with relatives, neighbors and friends.[5]

Within almost every family, the economic pressures on parents rob them of time with even their own children. Americans put in longer hours than workers in any other industrialized country, with many breadwinners working two or more jobs just to make ends meet.[6] With no adults at home, young children are relegated to day-care centers while older children are left in the company of video games, the Internet, or the corporate sponsors of their favorite television shows. According to a 2010 study of American children, the average 8- to 10-year old spends nearly eight hours a day with various media; older children and teenagers spend more than 11 hours a day with media. Not surprisingly, time spent in nature—essential for our well-being—has all but disappeared: only 10 percent of American children spend time playing outside on a daily basis.[7]

America's screen-obsessed children no longer have flesh-and-blood role models—parents and grandparents, aunts and uncles, friends and neighbors—to look up to. Instead, they have media and advertising images: rakish movie stars and music idols, steroid-enhanced athletes, airbrushed supermodels, and internet influencers. Children who strive to emulate the manufactured "perfection" of these role models are left feeling insecure and inadequate. This is one reason cosmetic surgery is increasing among America's children. According to the President of the American Academy for Facial Plastic Surgery, "the more consumers are inundated with celebrity images via social media, the more they want to replicate the enhanced, re-touched images that are passed off as reality." What's more, he adds, "we are seeing a younger demographic than ever before." [8]

It seems clear that "American culture" is no longer a product of the American people: it is instead an artificial consumer culture created and projected by corporate advertising and media. This consumer culture is fundamentally different from the diverse cultures that for millennia were shaped by climate, topography, and the local biota—by a dialogue between humans and the natural world. This is a new phenomenon: a culture determined by technological and economic forces, rather than human and ecological needs. It is not surprising that American children, even those who seem to "have everything", are so unhappy: like their parents, their teachers and their peers, they have been put on a treadmill that is ever more stressful and competitive, ever more meaningless and lonely.

As the globalization juggernaut continues to advance, the number of victims worldwide is growing exponentially. Millions of children from Mongolia to Patagonia are today targeted by a fanatical campaign to bring them into the consumer culture. The cost—measured in self-rejection, psychological breakdown, and violence—is massive. Like American children, they are bombarded with sophisticated marketing messages telling them that this brand of makeup will inch them closer to perfection, that brand of sneakers will make them more like their sports hero. But in the Global South—where the ideal is often blue-eyed, blonde, and Western—children are even more vulnerable. It's no wonder that sales of dangerous bleach to lighten the skin and contact lenses advertised as "the color of eyes you wish you were born with" are booming across the Global South. [9]

This psychological impoverishment is accompanied by a massive rise in material poverty. Even though more than 40 million Americans—nearly 13 percent of the population—live in poverty, [10] globalization aims to replicate the American model of development across the Global South. Among the results are the elimination of small farmers and the gutting of rural communities, with hundreds of millions of people drawn into sweatshops or unemployment in rapidly growing urban slums. Meanwhile, many of those whose ways of life are threatened by the forces of globalization are turning to fundamentalism, even terrorism.

The central hope of the American Dream—that our children will have a better life than we do— seems to have vanished. Many people no longer believe that our children really have any future at all.

Nonetheless, policymakers insist that globalization is creating a better world for everyone. How can there be such a substantial gap between the cheerleading rhetoric and the lives of real people?

Part of the disconnect results from the way globalization's promoters measure "progress". The shallowest definition compares the modern consumer cornucopia with what was available 50 or 100 years ago—as though electronic gadgets and plastic gewgaws are synonymous with happiness and fulfillment. More often the baseline for comparison is the Dickensian period of the early industrial revolution, when exploitation and deprivation, pollution and squalor were rampant. From this starting point, our child-labor laws and 40-hour workweek look like real progress. Similarly, the baseline in the Global South is the immediate post-colonial period, with uprooted cultures, poverty, over-population and political instability. Based on the misery of these contrived starting points, political leaders argue that our technologies and our economic system have brought a far better world into being. They assert that globalization will bring similar benefits to the "wretched, servile, fatalistic and intolerant human beings" in the remaining "undeveloped" parts of the world.

In reality, however, globalization is the continuation of a broad process that started with the age of conquest and colonialism in the Global South and the enclosures and the Industrial Revolution in the Global North. From then on, a single economic system has relentlessly expanded, taking over other cultures, other peoples' resources and labor. Far from elevating those people from poverty, the globalizing economic system has systematically impoverished them.

If there is to be any hope for a better world, it is vital that we connect the dots between "progress" and poverty. Erasing other cultures—

replacing them with an artificial culture created by corporations and the media they control—can only lead to an increase in social breakdown and poverty. Even in the narrowest economic terms, globalization means continuing to rob, rather than enrich, the majority. According to a 2017 report by Oxfam, the world's eight richest men now have more wealth than the poorest half of the global population combined. Their assets rose by more than $500 billion between 2010 and 2016, while the bottom 3.5 billion people became poorer by $1 trillion in that time.[11] This is globalization at work.

Because globalization systematically widens the gap between rich and poor, attempting in the name of equity to globalize the American standard of living is a fool's errand. The earth is finite, and global economic activity has already outstripped the planet's ability to provide resources and absorb wastes. When the average American uses 32 times more resources and produces 32 times more waste than the average resident of the Global South, it is a criminal hoax to promise that development can enable everyone to live the American Dream.

The spread of globalization has been profoundly destructive to people's ability to survive in their own cultures, in their own places on the earth. It has even been destructive to those considered to be its most privileged beneficiaries. Continuing down this corporate-determined path will only lead to further social, psychological and environmental breakdown. Whether they know it or not, America's children are telling us we need to go in a very different direction.

June 6, 2016

COSTS OF THE GREAT ACCELERATION
Alex Jensen

"The last 60 years have without doubt seen the most profound transformation of the human relationship with the natural world in the history of humankind",[1] concludes "The Great Acceleration", a major 2015 study of 24 indicators of human activity and environmental decline. We have all seen aspects of these trends, but to look at the study's 24 graphs together is to apprehend, at a glance, the totality of the monstrous scale and speed of modern economic activity. According to lead author W. Steffen, "It is difficult to overestimate the scale and speed of change. In a single lifetime humanity has become a planetary-scale geological force."[2]

Every indicator of intensity and scale of economic activity—from global trade and investment to water and fertilizer use, from pollution of every sort to destruction of environments and biodiversity—has shot up, precipitously, beginning around 1950. The graphs for every such trend point skyward still.

The Great Acceleration has manifested everywhere, including many areas not covered in the study. It is impossible to directly appreciate emotionally the ghastly scale of change. Only statistics can fully demonstrate the devastating consequences of our actions. For example:

- Humans now extract and move more physical material than all natural processes combined. Global material extraction has grown by more than 90 percent over the past 30 years, reaching almost 70 billion tons today.[3]

- During the 20th century, "global economic output expanded roughly 20-fold, resulting in a jump in demand for different resources of anywhere between 600 and 2,000 percent".[4]

- For more than 50 years, global production of plastic has continued to rise.[5] Today, around 300 million tons of plastic are produced globally each year. "About two thirds of this is for packaging; globally, this translates to 170 million tons of plastic created to be disposed of after one use." [6]

- The global sale of packaged foods has jumped more than 90 percent over the last decade, with 2012 sales topping $2.2 trillion. [7]

- "In the last 50 years, a staggering 140 million hectares... has been taken over by four industrial crops: soya bean, oil palm, rapeseed and sugar cane. These crops don't feed people: they are grown to feed the agro-industrial complex." [8]

Not only are the scale and speed of materials extraction, production, consumption and waste ballooning, but so too the scale and pace of the movement of materials through global trade. For instance, trade volumes in physical terms have increased by a factor of 2.5 over the past 30 years. In 2009, 2.3 billion tons of raw materials and products were traded around the globe. In the previous 20 years, maritime traffic on the world's oceans increased four-fold, causing more water, air and noise pollution on the open seas. [9]

While it may be correct, generically, to ascribe all these signs of the Great Acceleration to "humanity" or "human activity" as a whole, this ascription is also flawed. Indeed, the study concludes that the global economic system in particular has been a primary driver of the Great Acceleration. The graphs depicting economic activity (such as the amount of foreign direct investment or the number of McDonald's restaurants) and the ones charting environmental decline (such as biodiversity loss, forest loss, percentage of fisheries "fully exploited", etc.) look identical from a distance—both shooting dizzyingly upward since 1950. The resemblance is not coincidental: the latter are a consequence of the former.

This increase in global economic activity has been driven by the dynamics of capitalism and the pursuit of endless profits; by marketing and advertising; by subsidies and sops to industry of every stripe; and by the concomitant destruction of local, self-reliant communities around the world. In the process, much of "humanity" has been swept into the jetsam of the overall economic system. While this system may be the product of *some* human designs, to confuse it with humanity at large is to get the story backward.

One undeniable conclusion of all this, it seems to me, is that the increasing scale of economic activity—of "the economy"—is the heart of the multiple interlocking crises that plague societies and the earth today. The system's relentlessly expansionist logic is inimical to life, to the world, even to genuine well-being. If we wish to instead honor, defend, and respect life and the world, we must upend that logic and begin the urgent task of down-scaling economic activity and the system that drives it. We must embark upon the "Great Deceleration".

Nevertheless, from every organ of the establishment, where the commercial mind reigns, we hear that the challenge before us is not deceleration but *making the great acceleration even greater* by ramping up production and consumption still further. Even as governments insist solemnly on the need to arrest climate change and promote Sustainable Development Goals, they are handing over nearly boundless subsidies to industry, pushing for the expansion of global trade, and otherwise facilitating the acceleration of the acceleration.

Projections based on the assumption that the great acceleration will continue ad infinitum show, for example, that the number of cars will nearly double from 1.1 billion today to 2 billion by 2040; that seaborne trade will increase from 54 to 286 trillion ton-miles; that global GDP will climb from $69 trillion to $164 trillion; and so on. As a news article reporting the projections declares, "If there's a common theme, it's that there's going to be more of everything in the years ahead".[10] By 2025, the output of solid waste is expected to grow 70 percent, from 3.5 to more than 6 million tons per day.[11] Leaving aside the actual feasibility of such growth—given biophysical limits that are already well-surpassed—the very fact that the political and economic establishment takes such growth for granted and will continue to pursue it heedlessly is cause for grave concern.

In India, chemical and physical pollution has become so treacherous that it is deforming air and water into poisons to be avoided at the risk of health and life itself. Mephitic mountains of plastic waste choke every town and city, clog drains, suffocate rivers and shores, fill the stomachs of animals. Pesticides have killed soil and farmers alike across the country. Despite these and so many other manifestations of ecocide, industry and the government—central and state-level alike—clamor for more of it, faster. Because it is a "developing" country, we are told, the average Indian vastly *underconsumes* plastic, energy, cars, et al. Cultural traditions of thrift and sharing, wherever they still hang on, are seen as nettlesome but surmountable barriers to keeping the growth machine growing, faster. Replacing each and every one of those traditional practices with packaged, often disposable, commodities is an explicit goal of industry. Relentlessly generating novel needs is another. The current government's Make In India program, marketed to attract foreign investors and businesses, is the latest campaign to fuel this process.[12]

No matter how polluting, how much land and water are required, how many communities will be displaced and livelihoods destroyed, the formula is basically the same: more mines, more coal and power plants, more tourism, more of everything. For every industry, every product, every process that has swelled to become a planetary-scale abscess, the normal prescription that should obtain—"stop the swelling!"—is inverted. The out-of-control global economic system needs more and more growth just to feed and maintain itself.

In defense of this system, one may hear some version of the refrain: "These are the unfortunate costs we must pay to alleviate poverty, improve human well-being, and provide enough for all." This argument has become embarrassingly spurious. It is now widely known that not only has the great up-scaling bequeathed the planet and its inhabitants a legacy of destruction, ugliness, and waste, but its prodigious production and profit has failed to make a dent in the hunger and privation suffered by hundreds of millions. At the same time, it has unleashed a storm of junk food and diet-related diseases across the planet, which has persecuted the poor the worst.

Pollution, another consequence of the great acceleration, also harms the poor the worst. The great acceleration exacerbates poverty even as it churns the planet into money. Meanwhile, those most enriched in the process amount to a conference-room-sized group of individuals. The statistics will likely have grown even more outlandish by the time this is read: the world's 62 richest people own as much wealth as the poorest half of humanity.[13]

This system of plunder and inequality has, unsurprisingly, left in its wake demoralized human souls. The great acceleration and loneliness, depression, anxiety and estrangement are two sides of the same sinister coin; paralyzed and tyrannized by a surfeit of superficial "choice", by loss of meaning and connection, even the supposed beneficiaries of this system are miserable. [14]

What all this means is that the increasing scale and speed of the economy is, for the vast majority, the enemy of well-being. This fact offers some hope, for reducing the scale and speed of the economy suggests the possibility of relief and reclamation of contentment for those afflicted by affluence. Additionally, these changes would help to provide the actual material needs that are being trampled beneath the stampede of growth that is supposed to meet those needs. The great up-scaling is a sybaritic saturnalia for an infinitesimally small and incomprehensibly moneyed elite; it is everyone else's curse.

Excerpted from a 2019 essay titled "The Great Deceleration", The second half of this essay is in Chapter 5.

GLOBALIZATION PRODUCES SUSHI ... AND SLAVERY
Kristen Steele

It has been almost 160 years since President Abraham Lincoln's first Emancipation Proclamation, which led to the abolition of slavery in the United States. A century and a half later, most Westerners consider slavery a thing of the past, a relic of the colonial era. But in many parts of the "developing" world, globalization has picked up where colonialism left off. The slave-traders of old are today's human traffickers, and the profiteers in many cases are modern corporations.

According to estimates of the International Labor Organization of the United Nations, nearly 25 million people worked as slaves or in forced labor worldwide in 2016.[1] We hear most often about the women and children forced into the illegal sex trade. But both men and women are also sold to cotton and palm oil plantations, factories and fishing boats. Of these, palm oil production and overfishing in particular have received a lot of attention recently from the environmental and scientific communities. Often though, the human cost is overlooked.

"Forced labor represents the underside of globalization and denies people their basic rights and dignity," says Juan Somavia, director general of the International Labor Organization.

What's the connection to globalization? Globalization entails the dismantling of local economies and the destruction of livelihoods through centralization, unfair subsidies, and trade policies that favor big businesses over small. Production becomes geared towards export rather than for providing for local needs. In the "developing" world especially, these policies are driving small farmers into debt and eventually off the land. Without livelihoods to support themselves and their families, they are vulnerable to traffickers and their false promises of lucrative jobs.

Such was the case with Vannak Prum, a young Cambodian honored last year at the US State Department as a hero in the fight against human trafficking.[2] Eight years earlier, while seeking work to support himself and his pregnant wife, he was picked up by a trafficker on the Thai border and lured into a "job" in the fishing industry. For the next three years, he saw neither his family nor dry land, was drugged and forced to work 20 hours a day for no pay, and witnessed the brutal murders of fellow crew members who refused to follow orders. Finally, he managed to jump overboard off the coast of Malaysia and made his way to a police station, where he found himself promptly bundled off to another year of indentured servitude on a palm oil plantation. With so much profit involved and whole national economies at stake, governments frequently collude with the traffickers, funneling slaves from one industry to another.

Our gut instinct may be to shame governments, boycott Thai fish, or put pressure on snack food manufacturers to certify that their palm oil is free of human rights abuses. But while these measures of resistance help, we should also examine the global system that leads to these atrocities. It is facilitated by treaties and regulations, financed through subsidies, and driven by an unflagging commitment by most governments to increase GDP, whatever the costs to people or the planet.

For example, the Malaysian government gives more than half a billion dollars a year towards expanding palm oil production and exports, while arguing for the proposed Trans Pacific Partnership (TPP) under which "barriers to trade"—including regulations preventing the clearing of virgin rainforest for plantations or calling for fair wages and worker protection—would be eliminated. Meanwhile, fishing subsidies in Japan keep fish prices artificially low, encouraging overfishing and forcing other nations, like Thailand, to use slave labor to save costs in an effort to compete globally.

It's a messy package of debt, slavery, biodiversity loss, ecological destruction and corporate profits—all wrapped up and stamped with the unmistakable seal of economic globalization.

September 18, 2013. Some statistics have been updated.

SUPPLY CHAIN FAILURES
Helena Norberg-Hodge,
Henry Coleman and Steven Gorelick

Recent events have highlighted how vulnerable we are because of our dependence on the global economy. Long-distance supply chains are failing around the world, and the cost of living is skyrocketing as a result.

This is clearest when it comes to our most basic need of all: food. At the grocery store, Americans are paying 10 percent more for food than a year ago,[1] while the United Nations Food and Agriculture Organization reports that global food prices hit record highs in March.[2] In the United Kingdom, the price of chicken is set to soon match the price of beef.[3]

Why? Largely because economic globalization—which, in short, involves using public monies and government regulations to favor exports over self-reliance—has ensured that we source our food from ever farther away, via ever longer, more complicated supply chains.

That means that when China shuts down in response to COVID, it affects the whole world. When Russia invades Ukraine, global supplies of grains, vegetable oil and chicken feed are jeopardized. When energy prices rise, so do food prices, because industrial agriculture for export is built on fossil fuel-based fertilizers and fuel-guzzling transport. When synthetic fertilizer production facilities shut down because the price of fracked gas is too high, chemical-dependent farmers' yields fall.

And when fears grow, they snowball: Countries across the globe have halted food exports for fears of food insecurity.[4]

This would not be nearly so big a problem if the entire globe hadn't been made so dependent on global trade for basic needs. Consider the fact that global trade volume is now roughly 40 times greater than it was in 1950.[5] As governments—at the behest of global corporations— continue to subsidize and regulate in favor of global trade, people's lives and livelihoods are at the mercy of middlemen operating transnationally.

Thanks to globalization, food produced regionally or nationally is more likely to be exported than to feed the local population: they'll eat food imported from elsewhere. The situation is now so absurd that countries regularly import and export nearly identical quantities of identical products. In 2019, for example, the United States imported 1.53 million tons of beef, even as it exported 1.51 million tons.[6] In 2020, Germany was the world's top importer of butter ($851 million), and also the fourth-largest exporter of butter ($653 million).[7] That year, France both imported and exported about $1 billion worth of beef.[8] These are not outliers but typical examples of "redundant" trade in the global economy.

The list of actual and potential hiccups along these fragile supply chains is virtually endless. Those we have experienced recently include pandemic lockdowns, a blockage in the Suez Canal, and avian flu outbreaks. Last week, the Royal Bank of Canada reported that one-fifth of the global container ship fleet is currently stuck in congestion.

These are but harbingers of worse to come. The global food system itself—based as it is on chemical-intensive industrial monocultures for export—has decimated seed and livestock diversity, and is rapidly eroding topsoil and depleting fertility in our most important food bowls. Add to all this the fact that the global food system is responsible for up to 57 percent of all greenhouse gas emissions,[9] and widespread food system collapse is very possibly imminent.

Can we assume that these and other real-world effects will finally lead to a rethinking of "comparative advantage"—a cornerstone of the modern economy? The 1817 theory—an article of faith among supporters of "free trade" and globalization—asserts that if countries specialize in what they produce best and trade for every other need, all countries will be better off.

The theory of comparative advantage may have been plausible 200 years ago, but globe-spanning supply lines make no sense in our increasingly fragile world. During the pandemic, most countries would have been far better off had they relied more on local production, rather than on specialized production for global trade.

Unfortunately, political leaders on both left and right have ignorantly continued to promote economic globalization despite its mounting costs. Their policies have enabled multinational corporations and banks to accumulate immense wealth: by 2000, more than half of the largest economies in the world were corporations.[10] Their wealth

enables them to distort the democratic process through campaign dona-
tions and vast lobbying efforts, and to spend billions of dollars shaping
public opinion through advertising, data mining and media ownership.
Trade agreements even allow transnational corporations to sue governments if environmentally or socially conscious laws or regulations get in
the way of corporate profits. [11] In short, globalization has reshaped society in the interest of unaccountable, internationally mobile corporations.

For many rather obvious reasons, this is a bad idea. For example,
it is the main reason why governments have continuously failed to act
on the climate crisis. It is why profit-driven media have become ever
more polarizing and incendiary. It is why local businesses are being
driven to bankruptcy by global giants, and why communities are being
broken apart and amalgamated into ever-bigger, more anonymous,
more resource-intensive megacities. It is why billionaires continue to
get richer and richer, even as the majority of the world's people must
run ever harder and faster just to stay in place. As the resources needed
to fuel this globalized system become more scarce, conflict both within
and between countries is bound to rise.

The fact that these seemingly disparate issues are connected by their
shared roots in the globalizing economic system is, perhaps counterin-
tuitively, a reason for hope: by focusing on that root cause, we can begin
to identify systemic solutions that address all of those problems simultaneously. What's more, we can also see that these solutions are already
being pioneered by ordinary people all across the globe, acting with
little if any government support but on goodwill and common sense.

May 22, 2022

GLOBALIZATION AND TERROR
Helena Norberg-Hodge

For people in the modern world, there may be nothing more difficult to comprehend than the Islamic State, or ISIS. The beheadings, rapes, and other acts of cruelty seem beyond understanding, as does the wanton destruction of priceless ancient monuments. Perhaps most mystifying of all is the way ISIS has been able to recruit young men—and even some young women—from the industrialized West, particularly Europe. The conventional wisdom is that the cure for ethnic and religious violence is "development," education, and the opportunities provided by free markets. This seems not to be the case.

Because of the mainstream media's narrow and often misplaced focus, it's not surprising that most Westerners believe that religious extremism is primarily a problem of Islam. But the fighting in Syria and Iraq is not the only ethnic or religious conflict underway. There has been violence between Sinhalese and Tamils in Sri Lanka, Buddhists and Hindus in Bhutan, Hindus and Sikhs in Punjab, Eritreans and Ethiopians in the Horn of Africa, Hutu and Tutsi in Rwanda, ethnic Russians and Ukrainians in the former Soviet Union, and many more. The fact is, fanaticism, fundamentalism, and ethnic conflict have been growing for many decades—and not just in the Islamic world.

Failure to recognize this trend can lead to the belief that terrorism is a product of nothing more than religious extremism and will end when secular market-based democracies are established throughout the world. Unfortunately, the reality is far more complex, and, unless we address the underlying causes of conflict and terrorism, a more peaceful and secure future will remain elusive.

To really understand the rise of religious fundamentalism and ethnic conflict, we need to look at the deep impacts of the global consumer culture on living cultures throughout the planet. Doing so allows us not only to better understand ISIS and similar groups, but also to see a way forward that lessens violence on all sides.

My perspective comes from nearly fifty years of experience in numerous cultures in both the Global North and the Global South. I studied in Austria in 1966, when the Tyrol conflict was raging; I was a resident in Spain in the 1980s and 1990s, when the Basque separatist group ETA was active; I lived in England when pitched battles between Catholics and Protestants in Northern Ireland spilled over into bombings on the streets of London; and I've worked for almost four decades on the Indian subcontinent, where I've seen terrorist acts in Nepal as well as ethnic tensions and open conflict in India and Bhutan. Most importantly, I also witnessed firsthand the emergence of tensions between the Buddhist majority and the Muslim minority in Ladakh.

The Rise of Fundamentalism in Ladakh

For more than 600 years, Buddhists and Muslims lived side by side in Ladakh with no recorded instance of group conflict. They helped one another at harvest time, attended one another's religious festivals, and sometimes intermarried. In the past, Ladakhis would rarely identify themselves as Buddhists or Muslims, instead referring to their household or village of origin.

But with the heightened competition brought by development, that began to change. Political power, formerly dispersed throughout the villages, became concentrated in bureaucracies controlled by the Muslim-dominated state of Kashmir, of which Ladakh is part. In most countries the group in power tends to favor its own kind while the rest often suffer discrimination. Ladakh was no exception. Political representation and government jobs—virtually the only jobs available to formally-schooled Ladakhis—disproportionately went to Muslims. Thus, ethnic and religious differences—once largely ignored—began to take on a political dimension, causing bitterness and enmity on a scale previously unknown.

Young Ladakhis, for whom religion had been just another part of daily life, took exaggerated steps to demonstrate their religious affiliation and devotion. Muslims began requiring their wives and daughters to cover their heads with scarves. Buddhists in the capital began broadcasting their prayers over loudspeakers to compete with the Muslim prayer call. Religious ceremonies that were once celebrated by the whole community—Buddhist and Muslim alike—became instead occasions to flaunt one's wealth and strength. In 1987, tensions between the two groups exploded into violence. One mild-mannered Buddhist grand-mother, who a decade earlier had been drinking tea and laughing with her Muslim neighbor, told me, "We have to kill all the Muslims or they will finish us off."

Over the next few years, I met a number of young Ladakhis who also proclaimed that they were ready to kill people in the name of Islam or Buddhism. These were young men who hadn't had much exposure to the traditional teachings of their respective religions. Instead, they tended to be those who had studiously modeled themselves on Rambo and James Bond and who were the most psychologically insecure. On the other hand, those who managed to maintain their deeper connec-tions to the community and to their spiritual roots in general seemed psychologically strong enough to remain gentle and tolerant.

It may be surprising to some people to know that the Ladakhis most prone to violence were generally those with exposure to Western-style schooling. This feature of development—usually seen as unequivocally good—pulled the young away from the skills and values most suited to life on the Tibetan Plateau, substituting instead an education suited to a consumer lifestyle that will lie forever beyond the reach of the major-ity. Battered by the impossible dreams foisted on them by their schools, the media, and advertisements, many youth ended up unwanted, frus-trated, and angry.

Violence Around the World

Ladakh's story is not unusual. In Bhutan, a Hindu minority had co-ex-isted peacefully with a slightly larger number of Buddhists for an equally long period; fifteen years' exposure to outside economic pres-sures resulted in ethnic violence that left many people dead.[1] The rise of divisions, violence, and civil disorder around the world are predictable effects of forcing diverse cultures and peoples into a consumer mono-culture. The problem is particularly acute in the Global South, where people from many differing ethnic backgrounds are pulled into cities where they are cut off from their communities and cultural moorings and face ruthless competition for jobs and the basic necessities of life. In the intensely demoralizing and competitive situation they face, differences of any kind become increasingly significant, and tension between differing ethnic or religious groups can easily flare into violence.

In similar vein, Michel Chossudovsky, Professor of Economics at the University of Ottawa, argues that the ethnic cleansing in Kosovo in the 1990s had its roots at least partly in the macro-economic reforms imposed by Belgrade's external creditors such as the International Monetary Fund (IMF). Multi-ethnic Yugoslavia was once a regional industrial power with relative economic success. But after a decade of Western economic ministrations and five years of disintegration, war, boycott, and embargo, the economies of the former Yugoslavia lay in ruins. Chossudovsky writes:

> "In Kosovo, the economic reforms were conducive to the concurrent impoverishment of both the Albanian and Serbian populations contributing to fueling ethnic tensions. The deliberate manipulation of market forces destroyed economic activity and people's livelihood creating a situation of despair." [2]

Since rural communities and local economies in the Global North are being ripped apart by many of the same destructive forces at work in the Global South, it should be no surprise that the effects are similar there too. Christian fundamentalism, for example, has taken root in America's rural heartland, as has increased hostility toward immigrants, Muslims, and other ethnic minorities. Across Europe, there has been hostility towards immigrants and their children—not just the recent influx from Syria but also those who have been in Europe for decades. Many of these immigrants live on the tattered edges of glamorous cities whose affluence is like a cruel taunt. Moreover, neo-Nazi movements have gained strength in places like Greece, where the Golden Dawn party blames the country's economic woes on "illegal immigrants"—rather than on the "structural adjustments" that were the price for the latest bailouts. [3] At the same time, we can see—even in our own culture—that robbing men of self-respect and the ability to provide for themselves and their family is a recipe for violence. That violence is usually directed at "the other"—whether it's refugees, different religious or racial groups, or even women and children from their own community.

Despite the clear connection between the spread of the global monoculture and ethnic conflict, many in the West place responsibility at the feet of tradition rather than modernity, blaming "ancient hatreds" that have smoldered beneath the surface for centuries. Certainly, ethnic friction is a phenomenon that predates colonialism and modernization. But after four decades of documenting and analyzing the effects of globalization on the Indian subcontinent, I am convinced that becoming connected to the global consumer economy doesn't just exacerbate existing tensions—in many cases it actually *creates* them. The arrival of the global economy breaks down human-scale structures, destroys bonds of reciprocity and mutual dependence, and pressures the young to substitute their own culture and values with the artificial values of advertising and the media. In effect, this means rejecting one's own identity and rejecting one's self. In the case of Ladakh, it is clear that "ancient hatreds" didn't previously exist and cannot account for the sudden appearance of violence.

Lessening the Violence

The best long-term strategy to stop the spread of ethnic and religious violence is to reverse the policies that now promote growth-at-any-cost development. Today, free trade treaties—one of the prime engines of globalization—are pressuring governments to invest in ever larger-scale infrastructures and to subsidize giant, mobile corporations to the detriment of millions of smaller local and national enterprises. The creation of a global monoculture in the image of the West has proven disastrous on many counts, including the violence it does to cultures that must be pulled apart to accommodate the process.

Until about 500 years ago, local cultures throughout the world were the products of a dialogue between humans and a particular place; cultures grew from the bottom up and evolved in response to local conditions. They also absorbed and responded to outside influences such as trade, but the process of conquest, colonialism, and development that has affected so much of the world is fundamentally different: it has forcefully imposed change from the outside. And since the end of World War II, the forces dismantling local economies have grown far more powerful.

Today, speculative investment and transnational corporations are transforming every aspect of life—people's language, their music, their buildings, their agriculture, and their worldviews. That top-down form of cultural change works against diversity, against the very fabric of life.

It is vital that we in the West shift to a decentralized, less resource-intensive economic model immediately. But equally urgent is a shift in development policies for the less industrialized, less oil-dependent Global South, where a strategy based on decentralized, renewable energy would be far easier and less expensive to implement than continuing to pursue a centralized, carbon-intensive energy path. By improving conditions in villages, towns and small cities, this strategy would also help stem the unhealthy tide of urbanization—the depopulation of rural areas that is structurally linked to corporate-led globalization. We also need to look critically at even well-meaning proposals, like the UN's Sustainable Development Goals, that call for further "aid" to the Global South to alleviate poverty. The elimination of poverty is certainly a worthy goal, but most aid is export-oriented and actually increases real poverty while tying people more tightly to a global economy over which they have no control. It undermines the ability of communities and whole nations to produce for their own needs, maintain their own culture, and determine their own future. It cannot prevent either poverty or terrorism. Like further trade deregulation, most development aid primarily enables global corporations to exploit labor, resources, and markets worldwide.

What *is* needed is a shift away from globalization and towards economic localization, along with what I call "counter-development"— efforts that increase self-reliance while providing information to balance the romanticized images of the consumer culture disseminated by western style schooling and the media.

For forty years, Local Futures has been running a range of initiatives with those goals in mind. Paradoxically, these efforts have involved a closer connection between Westerners and people from the Global

South—we have even sponsored some to come on reality tours to the West. In Ladakh we have run programs that enable Westerners to experience traditional village life. The interest and involvement of these Westerners in Ladakh's culture and in farming has helped to counter the derogatory messages transmitted by Western media.

Working closely with indigenous leaders, our efforts have essentially been about countering and providing alternatives to global development models based on debt and fossil fuels. For this approach to be replicated, we urgently need major educational campaigns as well as closer dialogue between grassroots organizations in the Global North and the South. We need a movement that will lobby governments and the UN, making it clear that the most effective way for governments to contribute to a reduction in both poverty and violence is not to *scale up* funding for development but to *scale back* the forces of globalization.

Tragically, the primary "solutions" to the problem of terrorism have involved smart bombs, drone attacks, and wall-to-wall surveillance programs. At the same time, governments continue to undermine cultural identity through policies promoting a worldwide monoculture for the benefit of global corporations and banks. Such policies will only breed further desperation and fanaticism among people who already feel betrayed and disenfranchised. Encouraging instead a deeper dialogue between people in the Global North and South, while shifting our economic policies to support local and national economies, would set us on the path toward a more harmonious world.

July 29, 2015

HOW GLOBALIZATION LEADS TO AUTHORITARIANISM

Helena Norberg-Hodge

From Trump in America to Modi in India, from Le Pen in France to Duterte in the Philippines, from Brexit in the UK to the One Nation party in Australia, a swing to the political far-right is a worldwide phenomenon. In diverse parts of the globe, the same xenophobic rhetoric and prejudiced policies point to an underlying epidemic of fear and insecurity.

My 40 years' experience, working in both industrialized and land-based cultures, has made the primary reasons for this epidemic clear: competition has increased dramatically, job security is a thing of the past, and most people find it increasingly difficult to earn a livable wage. At the same time, identity is under threat as cultural diversity is replaced by a consumer monoculture worldwide. And as so often happens, insecure people point the finger of blame at the cultural "other".

The alarming rise of the far-right highlights the urgent need to identify the systemic roots of psychological insecurity, unemployment and rising poverty. And in order to do so, we need to look at the impact of globalization on communities around the world.

Globalization and Insecurity

People often associate globalization with international collaboration, travel and the spread of ideas. However, at its core, globalization is an *economic* process—one that has been at the heart of neoliberal ideology and the corporate agenda since the end of World War II. Economic globalization is the systematic deregulation of business and finance, primarily through trade treaties that give corporate entities the freedom to move across the world in search of the cheapest labor, the least stringent health and environmental standards, the biggest tax breaks and the most generous subsidies.

Over the last three decades, governments have unquestioningly embraced these "free trade" treaties. Not only do they enable corporations to move operations—and consequently jobs—wherever they please, they even give them the right to sue governments over laws or regulations that threaten their potential profits. Locked into a system requiring constant global "growth", communities have seen their local economies undermined, pulling them into dependence on a volatile corporate-led economy over which they have no control.

When we look at what is happening on the ground in both the "developed" and "developing" world, the structural connection between the globalizing economy and widespread insecurity becomes evident. The picture that emerges very clearly points to the neoliberal economy as the driver of fear, fundamentalism and political instability. In both the global North and South the enormous psychological and material insecurity fostered by globalization has greatly magnified the ability of demagogues to use fear and prejudice to manipulate public opinion.

To reverse this trend, neither a politics of identity nor of "left" versus "right" is sufficient. Instead, we need to change the structural economic forces at the root of the problem: in other words, we need to reverse the deregulation of global banks and corporations.

The trajectory of growing corporate power is not inevitable or natural, nor is it a consequence of supposed "efficiencies of scale", as many assume it to be. Rather, it is the result of decades of policy choices by national governments as well as international bodies like The World Bank and the IMF, which deliberately support the big and the global in the belief that corporate growth is the pathway to peace and prosperity. Not only have global corporations and banks been allowed to take advantage of differences in labor, health, safety, and environmental standards across the globe, they have also been granted huge tax breaks and massive direct subsidies. Even more insidiously, the corporate system has been built on a range of *indirect* subsidies—largely for the infrastructure on which globalization depends. The expansion of ports and mega-highways; the trillions of dollars governments given annually to subsidize fossil fuels; ever more advanced satellite communications technologies; an education system that trains people for jobs in the corporate world: these mechanisms structurally favor the big and global over the small and local, and most have been paid for not by the corporations themselves, but by the taxpayer.

In order to see how corporate deregulation has led to a breakdown of democracy, to the rise of far-right political leaders, and to increasing fundamentalism and violence, it is vitally important that we see the broader connections that mainstream analyses generally ignore.

Job Insecurity

As corporations are freed up, the jobs they provide become increasingly insecure. Under the first free trade treaty, the North American Free Trade Agreement (NAFTA), the USA suffered a net loss of an estimated 700,000 jobs as manufacturers relocated to Mexico, where wages were cheaper and standards lower.[1] Meanwhile, Mexico lost out too: highly subsidized agricultural products from the United States infiltrated local markets, undermining the livelihoods of approximately 2.3 million small farmers.[2] Many of these farmers were pulled from the land and ended up in Mexico's crowded cities, where they were forced to compete with one another for low-paying industrial jobs; with few viable options, many ended up migrating—legally or not—to the United States. These victims of globalization, ironically enough, often became the far-right's scapegoats for American job losses.

As globalization has proceeded, the disappearance of jobs has accelerated. For example, it is estimated that imports from China by Wal-Mart alone cost an estimated 400,000 American jobs between 2001 and 2013.[3]

While the media has emphasized rising standards of living among industrial workers in the global South, the benefits for workers there are heavily outweighed by the benefits to the corporations that offshore their manufacturing operations. Of the price paid for an Apple iPhone, for example, less than 2% (about $10) goes to the Chinese workers involved in its production, while 58% (almost $300) goes to Apple as profits.[4] Meanwhile, the increased wages earned by Chinese workers must be weighed against the Chinese government's suppression of workers' rights—which serves to depress wages (to the benefit of global corporations) while lowering workers' quality of life.[5]

It's not only the disappearance of jobs that leads to stagnant or declining standards of living, but the threat that jobs can be easily taken elsewhere if workers don't accept lower wages, longer hours or fewer benefits. The many multilateral and bilateral "free trade" treaties now in force serve to undercut workers' bargaining power, while multinational corporations benefit from what is commonly described as a "race to the bottom".

At the same time, jobs in the global economy are being systematically replaced by technology. This is a further price we pay for the immense scale of economic activity. While large-scale systems can afford investment in standardized, resource-intensive technologies, locally-adapted systems are inherently smaller and more diverse, and therefore cannot be efficiently operated by centralized technological systems.

In agriculture, for example, export-led markets demand huge amounts of standardized commodities; producing those foods on a large scale means monocultural production, which is heavily dependent on industrial machinery and chemical inputs—but requires only a relatively small agricultural labor force. On the other hand, local markets require a diversity of food products, which are best tended by human hands. In addition to providing far more jobs, small-scale, diversified production is far less taxing on local ecosystems, and can ensure sustainable livelihoods for many generations. However, as countries are pushed by deregulatory policies to open up to the global economy, small farms have given way to ever larger monocultures, and there have been massive declines in livelihoods in the agricultural sector from the UK to China.

The replacement of local jobs with centralized, energy-intensive technological systems is occurring in almost every sector of the economy. When a global corporation—propped up by a range of tax breaks and subsidies—enters a new market, the local economy tends to experience a net loss of jobs, as smaller competitors—more dependent on human labor—go out of business. Some studies have shown that every new supermarket in the UK entailed a net loss of 276 jobs. [6] The online marketer Amazon—seen as the pinnacle of technological efficiency—has destroyed 150,000 more jobs than it has created, according to a report from the Institute for Local Self-Reliance.[7] Like other online retailers, Amazon has not only benefited from communications and transport infrastructures built at public expense, it has avoided collecting state and local sales tax from its US customers—sales tax revenues that states and localities desperately need—giving Amazon a price advantage of as much as 9.75% over main street businesses.[8]

Political Insecurity

As the scale of the economy grows, people lose agency over their own lives. Transnational corporations have been encouraged by a deregulated banking system and a volatile stock market to grow endlessly, which they accomplish in part by gobbling up their smaller competitors. This has created a situation in which a handful of profit-making entities now monopolize global markets, and have grown bigger than nation states both in terms of wealth and political influence.

These multinationals have used their unprecedented power to lobby governments into still more economic deregulation. Most trade agreements include Investor-State Dispute Settlement (ISDS) clauses that grant foreign corporations the right to sue governments if a law or regulation might reduce their future profits. In 2014, for instance, Swedish nuclear power company Vattenfall sued Germany, seeking compensation for lost income after Germany announced it would phase out nuclear power following the 2011 nuclear disaster in Fukushima, Japan.[9] ISDS clauses are also used to attack public-interest regulations themselves. In 2009, the same Swedish power company sued Germany for €1.4 billion over power plant waste-water rules enacted by the City of Hamburg—regulations that Vattenfall claimed made its coal-fired power plant there unviable. Ultimately, the City of Hamburg was compelled by this ISDS suit to lower its environmental standards.[10]

"Free trade" clearly means freedom for the big players to do as they please. For the small players, however, it means quite the opposite: corporate influence over governments not only ensures that the multinationals are ever more deregulated, it also makes sure that their smaller, local and national competitors are *over*-regulated. From Washington to Delhi, from Paris to Santiago, governments have been lobbied by big business to constrain the activities of smaller businesses by locking them into unreasonable standards and convoluted bureaucracy. In many cases, an unfair burden falls on small-scale enterprises through regulations aimed at problems caused by large-scale production. Battery-style chicken farms, for example, clearly need significant environmental and health regulations: their millions of genetically-identical, closely confined animals are highly prone to disease, their tons of concentrated effluent need to be safely disposed of, and the long-distance transport of processed poultry entails the risk of spoilage. Yet a small producer—such as a farmer with a few dozen free-range chickens—is subject to essentially the same regulations, often raising costs to levels that make it impossible to remain in business. Large-scale producers can spread the cost of compliance over a far greater volume, making it appear that they enjoy "economies of scale" over smaller producers. Such discriminatory regulations are widespread: they are decimating farm-based cheese producers in Europe, local apple cider producers in the US, and small-scale food businesses in many other countries.

At the same time, governments themselves have been impoverished by corporate deregulation. Their funds have been stretched by the heavy subsidies handed out to attract big business, and their tax base has been eroded by tax breaks, offshoring, and the ability of multinationals to hide profits in countries with lower tax rates. Even worse, governments are left holding the bag for all the social and environmental problems—from workers displaced by outsourcing and downsizing, to the multiple effects of climate chaos—that are inevitable by-products of global growth.

With their financial situation deteriorating, many governments have been unable to meet the needs of their citizens. Increasingly distanced from the institutions where key decisions affecting their lives and livelihoods are made, and disenfranchised from their economic livelihoods, many people have become frustrated, angry, and disillusioned with the current political system. Although democratic systems worldwide have been hugely compromised by the de facto government of deregulated banks and corporations, most people blame their own government, often citing its inefficiencies and its inability to operate "like a business". Because they don't see the bigger picture, increasing numbers of people have grown susceptible to the false claims and empty promises of unconventional, authoritarian candidates, who are thereby able to gain a foothold in political arenas.

Psychological Insecurity

As local economies are undermined, the fabric of interdependence that holds communities together begins to unravel. This not only leads to social fragmentation and isolation, it also has the effect of lessening one's social security—a safety net previously founded on the assurance that the surrounding community could be relied upon for help in times of hardship.

At the same time, the global consumer culture that supports corporate growth is relentlessly expanding. People all over the world are targeted with advertising messages telling them: "you are not good enough as you are, but you can improve yourself by buying our product." As face-to-face relationships deteriorate and real-life role models are replaced by distant, artificial images of perfection in both mass-media and, increasingly, social media, unhealthy comparison runs rife. These trends are associated with rising rates of disorders such as anorexia, anxiety, aggression and even suicide, while social isolation, domestic stress and increasing economic pressures have given rise to epidemics of depression and addiction.

The glorification of modern, urban life in mass media around the world has been helping to pull people, especially young people, away from rural areas for many decades. This process has been exacerbated by the subsidizing of centralized, export-led markets, which systematically undermine the local economies of rural towns and villages. Dwindling economic and educational opportunities in these rural areas has meant decreasing populations, diminished cultural vitality, and fading prospects for the future. This is fertile ground for resentment, anger, and deepening psychological insecurity.

Left insecure and cut off from both community and the center of the new economy, people can be highly vulnerable to prejudice. In the global South especially, the breakdown of communities and cultures is severing rich intergenerational relationships and uprooting identities, often replacing them with unhealthy alternatives that reflect a desperate need for belonging.

Frustration, Confusion, and the Rise of Extremism

Despite the multitude of ways in which the global economic system deeply affects our lives, there has been little public discussion of its direction. This is hardly surprising, given that free trade treaties—the primary vehicle for corporate expansion—are negotiated in secret, not between democratically-elected representatives, but among corporate advisors. ISDS disputes, meanwhile, are settled in "kangaroo" courts, outside of the public legal system. The treaties themselves are thousands of pages long and extremely convoluted, and most parliamentarians only dimly understand the content, much less the real-world implications, of what they are signing onto.

In addition, most media outlets consistently fail to consider the root causes of our global crises, and instead largely focus on a theater of scandals and personalities, and on a left-right political dichotomy that no longer reflects the full spectrum of alternatives. There is little discussion of the invisible hand of global economic forces pressuring national governments worldwide. Even though there is a widespread distrust of multinational corporations, the lack of structural awareness has led farmers, small business owners and blue collar workers to believe that "big government" is the enemy. Tragically, they have been encouraged to embrace laissez-faire, free trade, neoliberal economics, despite the fact that these are the very policies harming all of these groups.

Because the bigger picture has been obscured, political conservatives blame left and green activists. You hear things like: "The unreasonable demands of labor unions is what forced industry out of the country." They blame the greens for having brought in environmental regulations that wrap small businesses in red tape, making it almost impossible for them to survive. The result is an increasing hatred of government in general, and of the left and green parties in particular.

Much of the public has become trapped in a demoralizing system of cutthroat competition that seems to intensify with each passing generation. It has become ever more difficult to hold onto a job, to pay the mortgage, to raise a family. Governments, meanwhile, are less able to provide health services or adequate educational opportunities. Because the role of policies favoring big business is rarely reported in the media, there is no check on those who point the finger of blame at immigrants, people of other religions, ethnicities or races, or government itself. In this confused situation, it's easy for fear-mongering, antagonism, and narrow-visioned authoritarian politics to emerge. Even in Scandinavia this process is underway, with Anders Breivik—the far-right extremist who killed 77 people in Norway—being the most extreme example.[12]

Challenging Authoritarianism

Having observed the acceleration of global corporate deregulation—and along with it the deterioration of the environment and the social fabric in multiple countries—it has become clear to me that it is the secrecy around the trade treaties that has allowed the global business giants to become so bloated and powerful at the expense of what people really care about. We urgently need widespread awareness of the big picture of economic deregulation and its impacts on our communities and personal lives. It is only because of blindness to this system that the nationalist pseudo-solutions of Trump, Brexit, Duterte and others have been able to gain strength, even as the global economic system has marched onwards, unfettered. Despite the fact that these right-wing political forces are often branded as "anti-globalist", they are actually serving to strengthen global monopolies; despite being described as "populist", they are further dividing us and exacerbating inequality.

Any movement to address the woes of the disenfranchised must not only expose and diagnose the systemic illness of economic deregulation, but must also present a coherent alternative. I believe that the path forward will involve a 180-degree turn-around in economic policy—from de-regulation towards re-regulation—so that business and finance become place-based and accountable to democratic processes. In short, we need to create a situation in which business and finance are shaped by the needs of civic society, rather than society being shaped by the needs of ever larger corporate conglomerates.

At the same time, we need to support the renewal of stronger, more diversified, self-reliant economies at the national, regional and local level. This is essential in order to restore the real economy—based in the natural world—which is being decimated by techno-economic structures that are erasing diversity, both biological and cultural. However, in order for these grassroots initiatives to really take off, they must be accompanied by fundamental policy shifts—not only the re-regulation of global corporations and banks, but also a shift in taxes and subsidies so that they no longer favor the big and the global but instead support small scale on a large scale. This implies a systemic shift in direction— from global to local.

May 5, 2018

3

DRIVERS OF THE GLOBAL SYSTEM

HUMAN NATURE: CAUSE OR CURE?
Helena Norberg-Hodge

T he documentary film *The Social Dilemma* was a wake-up call about how our opinions have been shaped by algorithms.[1] These have led us not only into increasingly antagonistic, polarized camps, but to remain uncritical of the mechanics of industrial development while accepting the notion that the root cause of our environmental and social crises is human nature itself.

The 1954 novel *Lord of the Flies*—which focused on the supposed dark heart of human nature—is still on the reading lists of most schools throughout the English-speaking world.[2] It tells the tale of marooned schoolboys' descent into tyranny, brutish exploitation of one another, and destruction of the natural environment.

But my observations not only of indigenous cultures but also of emerging trends at the grassroots worldwide, convince me that this is an inaccurate view of human nature. To me, it seems our true natures are compelling us to reject the path of competition and consumerism, and to forge systems based on cooperation and care.

A real-life version of *Lord of the Flies*—unearthed by Rutger Bregman in his landmark book *Humankind: a Hopeful History*—backs me up.[3] When six schoolboys from Tonga really did get stranded on an uninhabited island for 15 months, they did not try to kill or dominate one another, but rather cooperated diligently, built gardens, nursed each other through injury, and even fashioned musical instruments from the parts of their broken boat.

The slandering of human nature as innately greedy, uncaring and cruel has deep roots in Western culture. This view is even held by environmental and social activists who, ignorant to the way the global economic system has precipitated today's crises, believe innate human greed is to blame. They have become convinced that plastic-filled oceans, modern-day slavery, rising greenhouse emissions and other crises are all because of us—"the consumers"—who consume without a second thought about workers or the environment.

But the truth is that unethical, unsustainable choices have been thrust upon us. Because our governments have systematically deregulated and subsidized huge global corporations, we have been separated further and further from the sources of our sustenance, robbing us of the ability to comprehend our impacts on other people or the natural world.

If the root cause of our many crises were human nature, there is little we can do about it. But if economic structures are to blame, there is a solution: we need to change the economic system. How? By changing government policy so that it no longer subsidizes and regulates in favor of global monopolies, but in support of local businesses and place-based industries. These smaller economic structures are more sustainable and humane, simply because they are able to respond to the unique needs of the diverse communities and ecosystems in which they operate. Their human scale also makes it easier for us to see the impacts of the choices business make, leaving them far more accountable.

Part of you may doubt whether it's possible to change the economy, but another part of you—a growing part, perhaps—will recall that the current global economy has existed for scarcely more than a few hundred years—a tiny blip on our 200,000-year evolution. Your body will remember you're not built for competitive consumerism—you're designed for a life connected to others and to the natural world.

The more we experience the emptiness, competition and isolation of the "show-off" consumer culture, the more our intuition leads us in the direction of localized connection. In this way, human nature might just be our best guide towards kinder and more sustainable economic systems.

We are seeing the growth of a worldwide movement that, against the odds, is rebuilding local food systems, strengthening local businesses, and reweaving the bonds of deep community. From the food sovereignty movement and the rise of farmers' markets to the success of group-oriented and nature-based therapies like therapeutic horticulture and twelve-step programs, people are localizing in common-sense, intuitive ways.

When you see the world through a global-to-local lens, you see a world simultaneously moving in two different directions. On the one hand, the top-down pressures of a machine-like economic system are sustained by blindness, polarization, and a misinformed view of human nature.

On the other hand, an intuitive yearning for a kinder and more sustainable world represents a perennial and synergetic power. It is the power of human nature rising up to re-establish the interdependent webs of relationships that have informed our evolution and make us who we really are.

June 5, 2021

THE MARCH OF THE MONOCULTURE
Helena Norberg-Hodge

For many, the rise of the global economy marks the final fulfillment of the great dream of a "Global Village". Almost everywhere you travel today you will find multi-lane highways, concrete cities and a cultural landscape featuring gray business suits, fast-food chains, Hollywood films and cellular phones. Even in the remotest corners of the planet, Barbie, Lady Gaga, and the Marlboro Man are familiar icons. From Cleveland to Cairo to Caracas, Disney is entertainment, and CNN is news.

The world, we are told, is being united by virtue of the fact that everyone will soon be able to indulge their desire for a Westernized, urbanized consumer lifestyle. West is best, and joining the bandwagon brings closer a harmonious union of peaceable, rational, democratic consumers "like us".

This worldview assumes that it was the chaotic diversity of cultures, values, and beliefs that lay behind the conflicts of the past: as these differences are removed, the differences between us will be resolved.

As a result, around the world villages, rural communities and their cultural traditions are being destroyed on an unprecedented scale by globalizing market forces. Communities that have sustained themselves for hundreds of years are simply disintegrating. The spread of the consumer culture seems unstoppable.

Creating the Consumer Monoculture

Historically, the erosion of cultural integrity was a conscious goal of colonial developers. French government adviser on colonial affairs D. Goulet, for example, urged that "traditional peoples must be shocked into the realization that they are living in abnormal, inhuman conditions as psychological preparation for modernization". Or, as applied anthropologist Ward Goodenough explained:

"The problem is one of creating in another a sufficient dissat-isfaction with his present condition of self so that he wants to change it. This calls for some kind of experience that leads him to reappraise his self-image and re-evaluate his self-esteem." [1]

Towards this end, change agents were advised that they should:

1. "Involve traditional leaders in their programs.
2. Work through bilingual, acculturated individuals who have some knowledge of both the dominant and the target culture.
3. Modify circumstances or deliberately tamper with the equilibrium of the traditional culture so that change will become imperative.
4. Attempt to change underlying core values before attacking superficial customs." [2]

It is instructive to consider the actual effect of these strategies on the well-being of individual peoples in the Global South. For example, the Toradjas tribes of the Poso district in central Celebes (now Sulawesi, Indonesia) were deemed completely incapable of "development" without drastic intervention. Writing in 1929, A.C. Kruyt reported that the happiness and stability of Toradjas society was such that "development and progress were impossible" and that they were "bound to remain at the same level". [3]

Toradja society was cashless, and there was neither a desire for money nor the extra goods that might be purchased with it. In the face of such contentment, mission work proved an abject failure as the Toradjas had no interest in converting to a new religion, sending their children to school or growing cash crops. So, in 1905, the Netherlands Indies government decided to bring the Poso region under firm control, using armed force to crush all resistance. As a result of relocation and continual government punishment and harassment, mortality rates soared among the increasingly desperate and bewildered Toradjas. Turning to the missionaries for help, the Toradjas converted to Christianity and began sending their children to school. Eventually they began cultivating coconut and coffee plantations and acquired new needs for oil lamps, sewing machines, and "better" clothes. The self-sufficient tribal economy had been superseded as a result of deliberate government action.

In many countries, schooling was the prime coercive instrument for tampering with "underlying core values" and proved to be a highly effective means of destroying self-esteem, fostering new needs, creating dissatisfactions, and generally disrupting traditional cultures. An excerpt from a French reader designed in 1919 for use by French West African school-children gives a flavor of the kinds of pressures that were imposed on children: "It is... an advantage for a native to work for a white man, because the Whites are better educated, more advanced in civilization than the natives... You who are intelligent and industrious, my children, always help the Whites in their task. That is a duty." [4]

Cultural Erosion Today

As wealth is transferred away from nation states into the rootless casino of the financial markets, the destruction of cultural integrity is now far subtler than before. Most corporate and government executives no longer consciously plan the destruction they wreak—indeed they are often unaware of the consequences of their decisions on real people on the other side of the world. This lack of awareness is fostered by the cult of specialization that pervades our society: the job of a public relations executive is confined to producing business-friendly sound bites while time constraints and a narrow focus prevent a questioning of their broader impacts. The tendency to undermine cultural diversity proceeds on autopilot as an inevitable consequence of the spreading global economy.

But if the methods employed by the masters of the "Global Village" are less brutal than in colonial times, the scale and effects are often even more devastating. The digital revolution has helped to speed up and strengthen the forces behind the march of a global monoculture, which is now able to disrupt traditional cultures with a shocking speed and finality that surpasses anything the world has witnessed before.

Preying on the Young

Today, Western consumer conformity is descending on the less-industrialized parts of the world like an avalanche. "Development" brings tourism, Western films and products, and, more recently, satellite television and smartphones to the remotest parts of the earth. All provide overwhelming images of luxury and power. Adverts and action films give the impression that everyone in the West is rich, beautiful, and brave, and leads a life filled with excitement and glamour.

In the commercial mass culture that fuels this illusion, advertisers make it clear that Westernized fashion accessories equal sophistication and being "cool". In diverse "developing" nations around the world, people are induced to meet their needs not through their community or local economy but by trying to "buy in" to the global market. People are made to believe that, in the words of a US advertising executive in China, "imported equals good, local equals crap."

Even more alarming, people end up rejecting their own ethnic and racial characteristics—they feel shame in being who they are. Around the world, blonde-haired blue-eyed Barbie dolls and thin-as-a-rake cover girls set the standard for women. Already now, seven-year-old girls in Singapore are suffering from eating disorders, and it is not unusual to find East Asian women with eyes surgically altered to look more European, dark-haired Southern European women with hair dyed blonde, and Africans with blue- or green-colored contact lenses aimed at "correcting" dark eyes.

The one-dimensional, fantasy view of modern life is a slap in the face for young people in the Global South. Teenagers in particular come to feel ashamed of their traditions and their origins. The people they learn to admire and respect on television tend to be "sophisticated" city dwellers with fast cars and designer clothes, spotlessly clean hands and shiny white teeth. Yet they find their parents asking them to choose a way of life that involves working in the fields and getting their hands dirty for little or no money, and certainly no glamour. It is hardly surprising, then, that many choose to abandon the old ways of their parents for the siren song of a Western material paradise.

For millions of youths in rural areas of the world, modern Western culture appears vastly superior to their own. They see incoming tourists easily spending $100 a day—the equivalent of a visitor to the US spending $5,000 a day. Besides promoting the illusion that all Westerners are multi-millionaires, tourism and media images also give the impression that we never work—since for many people in the "developing" world, sitting at a desk or behind the wheel of a car does not constitute work.

People in the "less developed" parts of the world are not aware of the negative social or psychological aspects of Western life so familiar to us: the stress, the loneliness, the fear of growing old, the rise in clinical depression and other "industrial diseases" like cancer, stroke, diabetes and heart problems. Nor do they see the environmental decay, crime, poverty, homelessness and unemployment. While they know their own culture inside out, including all of its limitations and imperfections, they see only a glossy, exaggerated side of life in the West.

The Pressure to Modernize in Ladakh

My own experience amongst the people of Ladakh is a clear, if painful, example of the destruction of traditional cultures by the faceless consumer monoculture. When I first arrived in the area in 1975, the vast majority of Ladakhis were self-supporting farmers, living in small, scattered settlements in the high desert. Though natural resources were scarce and hard to obtain, the Ladakhis had a remarkably high standard of living, with beautiful art, architecture and jewelry. Life moved at a gentle pace and people enjoyed a degree of leisure unknown to most of us in the West. Most Ladakhis only really worked for four months of the year, and poverty, pollution, and unemployment were alien concepts.

That year, I remember being shown around the remote village of Hemis Shukpachan by a young Ladakhi named Tsewang. It seemed to me, a newcomer, that all the houses I saw were especially large and beautiful, and I asked Tsewang to show me the houses where the poor lived. He looked perplexed for a moment, then replied, "We don't have any poor people here."

In recent years, external forces have caused massive and rapid disruption in Ladakh. Contact with the modern world has debilitated and demoralized a once-proud and self-sufficient people, who today are suffering what can best be described as a cultural inferiority complex.

In traditional Ladakhi culture, virtually all basic needs—food, clothing and shelter—were provided without money. Labor was free of charge, part of an intricate and long-established web of human relationships. Because Ladakhis had no need for money, they had little or none. However, when they saw outsiders—tourists and visitors—spending what was to them vast amounts of cash on inessential luxuries, they suddenly felt poor. Not realizing that money was essential in the West—that without it people often go homeless or even starve—they didn't recognize its true value. They began to feel inadequate and backward. Eight years after Tsewang had told me the Ladakhis had no poverty, I overheard him talking to some tourists: "If you could only help us Ladakhis", he was saying, "we're so poor."

Tourism is part of the overall process of development that the Indian government is promoting in Ladakh. The area is being integrated into the Indian, and hence the global, economy. Subsidized food is imported from the outside, while local farmers, who had previously grown a variety of crops and kept a few animals to provide for themselves, have been encouraged to grow cash crops. In this way, they are becoming dependent on forces beyond their control—huge transportation networks, oil prices, and the fluctuations of international finance. Over the course of time, inflation obliges them to produce more and more to secure the income that they now need in order to buy what they used to produce themselves. Individual Ladakhis once wielded real influence and power within their own village-scale economy. Now each is just one within a national economy of more than a billion and within a global economy of over 7 billion. Their influence and power have been reduced to zero.

As a result of external investments, the local economy is crumbling. For generation after generation, Ladakhis grew up learning how to provide themselves with clothing and shelter; how to make shoes out of yak skin and robes from the wool of sheep; how to build houses out of mud and stone. As their building traditions give way to "modern" methods, the plentiful local materials are left unused while competition for a narrow range of modern materials—concrete, steel and plastic—skyrockets. The same thing happens when people begin eating identical staple foods, wearing the same clothes and relying on the same finite energy sources. For global corporations, making everyone dependent on the same resources creates efficiency; but for consumers it creates artificial scarcity and heightens competitive pressures.

As they lose the sense of security and identity that springs from deep, long-lasting connections to people and place, the Ladakhis are starting to develop doubts about who they are. In the traditional village, where everyone wore essentially the same clothes and looked the same to the casual observer, there was more freedom to relax. As part of a close-knit community, people felt secure enough to be themselves. The images they now get from outside tell them to be different from their peers, to own more, to buy more and thus be "better" than they are. The previously strong, outgoing women of Ladakh have been replaced by a new generation that is unsure of themselves and desperately concerned with their appearance.

And as their desire to be "modern" grows, Ladakhis are turning their backs on their traditional culture. I saw Ladakhis wearing wristwatches they could not read and heard them apologizing for the lack of electric lighting in their homes—electric lighting which, in 1975 when it first appeared, most villagers laughed at as an unnecessary gimmick. Even traditional foods are no longer a source of pride: now, when I'm a guest in a Ladakhi village, people apologize if they serve the traditional roasted barley, *ngamphe*, instead of instant noodles.

Ironically, modernization—so often associated with the triumph of individualism—has produced a loss of individuality and a growing sense of personal insecurity as people feel pressured to conform and to live up to an idealized image of who they should be.

While the myth makers of the Global Village celebrate values of togetherness, the disparity in wealth between the world's upper income brackets and the 90 percent of people in the poor countries represents a polarization far more extreme than existed in the 19th century. Use of the word "village"—intended to suggest relative equality, belonging and harmony—obscures a reality of high-tech islands of privilege and wealth towering above oceans of impoverished humanity struggling to survive. The global monoculture is a dealer in illusions. While promising a glittering, wealthy lifestyle, it can never provide for the majority: it is destroying the sustainable ways of living that traditions and local economies provided. For what it destroys, the global monoculture provides no replacement but a fractured, isolated, competitive and unhappy society.

March 15, 1999

ICE CREAM, SHAMANS, AND CLIMATE CHANGE
Steven Gorelick

I n the summer of 1969, I was 18 years old with a job driving an ice cream truck in a small New England town. One July afternoon, the weather was hot and humid—ideal for ice cream—but business was dismal, the streets almost deserted. Eventually someone ran out and flagged me down, but he wasn't interested in ice cream: "Come in the house!" he yelled, "it's happening now!" I knew immediately what he meant: the first lunar landing was under way, and Neil Armstrong was about to step onto the moon. I spent the next several hours in a stranger's house, glued to the TV like millions of others around the world.

Along with the grainy lunar footage and the clipped banter between the astronauts and mission control, what I most remember from that day involved the reactions of the world's political and religious leaders. Most of the congratulatory messages were a monotonous mix of pride in human achievement and pleas for America to use its foothold on the moon for peaceful purposes. But there was a surprising exception: a shaman from somewhere in Africa (my memory yields neither name nor country) declared that the project was a huge mistake because "walking on the moon will change the weather." The news anchor seemed to suppress a smile as he read the statement, and I remember thinking how neatly it reflected the difference between the benighted, superstitious world we were leaving behind and the bright technological future we were about to enter.

Since then, my thinking on both indigenous worldviews and high technology has changed dramatically. One reason is that the shaman was right.

The weather has, in fact, changed. Human-induced global warming is accepted by almost everyone but fossil-fuel executives and the most credulous denizens of the internet. *But climate change has nothing to do with landing a man on the moon*, I can hear you say. In a narrow sense, that's true, but I don't believe the shaman was thinking narrowly.

As Edward Goldsmith points out in his seminal book, *The Way*, indigenous worldviews commonly hold that humans have a proper place in the cosmic hierarchy, and when they violate that order, they bring misfortune to themselves, their families, their communities, the local environment, the world, and to the cosmos itself. Stepping on the moon was, in the eyes of the shaman, an irresponsible act of hubris and disrespect for the natural order.

For those unconvinced by indigenous belief systems, here's a more "rational" way to look at it. Sending a man to the moon required huge infrastructures for extracting, refining, and transporting energy and other resources, as well as for educational and research institutions that advanced and perfected the many technologies needed for space travel. All these in turn had to be funded by surpluses from an immense centralized economy—one that required tremendous amounts of resources and gave rise to equally tremendous amounts of pollution. Even my lowly ice cream truck was part of that economy, helping generate the wealth (and taxes) needed to hoist a man all the way to the moon and back. That truck, not coincidentally, also spewed a lot of greenhouse gases.

In other words, any society capable of putting a man on the moon must have an economy so massive that—as the shaman suggested—it is bound to bring misfortune to family, community, local ecosystems, and the biosphere. This is especially true when that economy is wedded to a reductionist scientific and technological worldview that holds nothing sacred and is thus able (and willing) to manipulate and commodify everything—even the building blocks of life and matter. This is, of course, a description of today's global economy.

As we consider our response to the disturbing reality of climate change, we would do well to think broadly, like that African shaman. In this light, climate change is *not* the most serious problem we face; it is instead the most serious *symptom* of a larger problem. Other symptoms include the destruction of rainforests, the depletion of topsoil and groundwater, pesticide residues in everything from mother's milk to polar bear fat, the growing gap between rich and poor, dead zones and floating garbage islands in the oceans, religious fundamentalism and ethnic conflict, the erosion of democracy, the epidemic of depression, and much more.

All of these symptoms emanate from the same source: a techno-economic system designed to meet the profit and growth demands of corporations and banks. This same system is eroding cultural diversity and individual identity by pulling every last one of us into an unsustainable globalized consumer culture; a system that creates insatiable desires—including the desire for the latest technological "innovation"—but fails to meet our real needs for connection to community and the natural world.

As I hope the African shaman would agree, merely switching from fossil fuels to "clean energy" will be insufficient to address climate change, and it won't alleviate the many other signs of breakdown. Rather than just changing the fuel that runs this destructive economic system, we need to change the system itself. And rather than continuing to deepen our exploitation of the natural world, we need to acknowledge its sacredness and approach it with humility.

September 14, 2014

WHAT IS EDUCATION FOR?
Steven Gorelick

Almost everywhere, the public applauds investments in education. Literacy statistics, high school graduation rates and per capita spending on schools are often used as yardsticks of national enlightenment. Education is considered so crucial to societal well-being that most countries make the formal schooling of their children compulsory. Given the importance attached to education, it's reasonable to ask what its function is.

First of all, the modern educational system is a *homogenizer*, with the goal of ensuring that children are all molded into roughly the same shape before leaving school. In a sense this is not so different from the role education has played in traditional cultures. Anthropologist Margaret Mead described education as, "the cultural process... in which each new born individual is transformed into a full member of a specific human society" [1] —a definition that could be applied equally well to hunter-gatherers and to modern urbanites. But Mead's reference to *specific* human societies is crucial: each culture is unique in its environment, local resources, and cultural history, and, consequently, an appropriate education will naturally differ from place to place.

Today, however, a single societal model is forcing itself into every corner of the planet; in the process, it is helping to homogenize diverse cultures and to erase the adaptations that connect people to their local circumstances. In the monocultural global economy, there is little room for educational diversity; instead, a one-size-fits-all curriculum is uniformly applied. This homogeneity is one reason schools are "institutions which more and more resemble one another, like airports and motels", in the words of Wendell Berry.[2]

This is particularly destructive in the Global South, where modern schooling systematically erases centuries of accumulated location-specific knowledge. Helena Norberg-Hodge describes traditional education in Ladakh, where children learned from parents, grandparents and older siblings how to thrive in their particular environment:

"Helping with the sowing, for instance, they would learn that on one side of the village it was a little warmer, on the other side a little colder. From their own experience children would come to distinguish between different strains of barley and the specific growing conditions each strain preferred. They learned to recognize even the tiniest wild plant and how to use it, and how to pick out a particular animal on a faraway mountain slope.... Education was location-specific and nurtured an intimate relationship with the living world. It gave children an intuitive awareness that allowed them, as they grew older, to use resources in an effective and sustainable way." [3]

Modernization, on the other hand, brought with it a very different form of education:

"...modern schooling acts almost as a blindfold, preventing children from seeing the context in which they live. They leave school unable to use their own resources, unable to function in their own world.... School is a place to forget traditional skills and, worse, to look down on them.... The basic curriculum is a poor imitation of that taught in other parts of India, which is itself an imitation of British education. There is almost nothing Ladakhi about it." [4]

When imposed on largely self-reliant communities and their economies, modern schooling severs a link in the chain by which knowledge was passed from generation to generation—knowledge that enabled people to sustain themselves from local resources.

The globalized standard to which modern education aspires is, however, well-suited to the needs of corporations. These companies use similar methods to produce goods that are meant to be purchased by similar consumers everywhere in the world. Thus, formal schooling in Indonesia teaches students little about indigenous knowledge and the sustainable use of local resources, but it does prepare them well enough to assemble sneakers in a Nike factory, to respond to advertising messages that influence their spending habits, and to count it all as "progress".

It is not only in the South that formal schooling separates children from their local context. John Taylor Gatto, who spent 26 years as an award-winning teacher in New York City's public school system, has described what his seventh-grade students know:

> "My kids don't know what a mile is, not really, although I think they could pass a test on it; in similar fashion they don't know what democracy is, or what money is, or what an economy is, or how to fix anything. They've heard of Mogadishu and Saddam Hussein but they couldn't tell you the name of the tree outside their window if their life depended on it.... Some of them can do quadratic equations, but they can't sew a button on a shirt or fry an egg; they can bubble in answers with a number two pencil but they can't build a wall." [5]

Learning the Industrial Worldview

Homogenizing children worldwide also means imbuing them all with the *worldview of industrialism*. Among other things, that worldview is highly scientific and reductionist, and values empirical "facts" above all other forms of knowledge. As David Orr notes, "the architects of the modern worldview, notably Galileo and Descartes, assumed that those things that could be weighed, measured, and counted were more true than those that could not be quantified. If it could not be counted, in other words, it did not count." [6]

This emphasis on the scientifically measurable reduces nature to clusters of matter interacting in obedience to the laws of physics; deprived of intrinsic value, nature's worth is determined only by what it provides for human use. This is the Enlightenment attitude articulated nearly 400 years ago by Francis Bacon, father of the scientific method, whose goal was "to establish the power and dominion of the human race itself over the universe". [7] Bacon's ideological descendants in the scientific/educational establishment continue to pursue that goal today—in part through oxymoronic disciplines like "Wildlife Management", through reputable scientific papers devoted to "Managing Planet

Earth", [8] and through concerted efforts to alter, for human ends, the genome of the living world.

An education consistent with the modern worldview is compartmentalized into disciplines that are separate and seemingly independent. Through the fragmented lens of specialized knowledge, problems appear as isolated symptoms while root causes are obscured—especially when revealing them would challenge the assumptions underpinning the industrial model. "In this way", Edward Goldsmith argues,

> "the world-view of modernism prevents us from understanding
> our relationship with the world we live in and adapting to it....
> Instead modernism, and the paradigms of science and econom-
> ics in particular, serve to rationalise economic development or
> 'progress'—the very behaviour that is leading to the destruction
> of the natural world....[9]

A narrow, fragmented perspective also allows individuals to avoid confronting the consequences of their actions. Even well-intentioned people—many of whom are earnestly concerned about humanity and the environment—nonetheless work for corporations or institutions involved in the rawest forms of human and environmental exploitation. A Union Carbide employee that looks no further than the increased "productivity" pesticides provide can be blind to the impacts on human health, the environment, and the livelihoods of small farmers. A World Bank employee focused closely on per capita income or the availability of electricity can neglect the breakdown of cultures, communities, and ecosystems that Bank policies cause. Scientific specialists can devote their working lives to technologies ranging from atomic weaponry to cloned sheep, while the consequences are neatly compartmentalized into subject headings marked "national defense" or "scientific curiosity". For such people, many years of specialized training has narrowed their focus so tightly that the broader effects of their work are all but invisible to them.

Promoting Technophilia

The educational system also reinforces the notion that *viable societies must be based upon the industrial model.* Despite its many flaws, the "normalcy" of this model is rarely questioned by the educational establishment. As Edward Goldsmith makes clear:

> "... *the modern discipline of economics is based on the assumption that the destructive economic system that is operative today is normal; the discipline of sociology on the assumption that our modern atomized and crime-ridden society is normal; our political science on the assumption that the elected dictatorships that govern modern nation states are normal; and our agricultural science on the assumption that large-scale, mechanized, chemical-based agriculture (which rapidly transforms arable land into desert) is normal. It simply does not occur to many academics that what they take to be normal is very atypical in the light of humanity's total experience on this planet...*" [10]

Since its baseline is firmly drawn in the industrial era, modern education focuses far more on the workings of the technosphere than the biosphere. The implicit message is that life itself ultimately depends on technology and human-made institutions, not on the natural world. A Yale University economist thus dismissed the impact of global warming on the US since "climate has little economic impact upon advanced industrial societies":

> "*Cities are increasingly becoming climate proofed by technological changes like air-conditioning and shopping malls.... Studies of the impact of global warming on the United States and other developed regions find that the most vulnerable areas are those dependent on unmanaged ecosystems—on naturally occurring rainfall, run-off and temperatures, and the extremes of these variables.... Most economic activity in industrialized countries, however, depends very little on the climate. Intensive care units of hospitals, underground mining, science laboratories, communications, heavy manufacturing and microelectronics are among the sectors likely to be unaffected by climatic change. In selecting whether to*

set up in, say, Warsaw or Hong Kong, few businesses will
consider temperature a weighty factor." [11]

In this view, the world inhabited by industrialized peoples is so divorced from nature that major disruptions to the biosphere would scarcely be noticed. Disruptions to the technosphere, on the other hand, would be catastrophic: "There is no life today without software", an executive of a major US-based corporation claimed. Without computers, "the world would probably just collapse". [12]

As David Orr has observed about modern schooling, faith in technology "is built into nearly every part of the curriculum as a kind of blind acceptance of the notion of progress" [13]. But corporations also use the educational infrastructure to gain acceptance for the specific technologies they control. This is particularly true in America, where corporations provide cash-starved schools with free study materials and teacher's kits laden with corporate-friendly messages. Monsanto, the corporation responsible for biotechnologies ranging from Round-up-ready soybeans to genetically-engineered bovine growth hormone, recently gave an "environmental" award to company employees who devised a "student education project ... that worked to raise student awareness about environmental benefits from biotechnology." [15] Along with seed corporation Pioneer Hi-Bred International, Monsanto also underwrote "Field of Genes", a classroom curriculum for teachers that gives an industry spin on genetics, biotechnology, and genetic engineering.[16] Similarly, the timber-industry giant Weyerhauser created a teacher's guide that suggests students discuss the "innovative practices" Weyerhauser has introduced to forest management.[17]

Training for Roles in a Corporate Economy

A further function of the modern educational system is to *prepare children and young adults for jobs in a corporate-dominated global economy.* Even corporations readily admit that they depend on the educational infrastructure to churn out their labor force. Eminent European chemists issued a report concluding that Europe's chemical industry would relocate to another part of the world unless research received more government support. One of the report's authors noted that "*industry is reliant on universities for its workforce,* so we must ensure that academic institutions are properly funded" (emphasis added).[18]

Having grown wealthier than many governments, corporations are increasingly willing to pay for the right to tailor educational infrastructure to their specific needs. Corporations endow university chairs, pay for the construction of buildings and research facilities, and fund whole departments in fields useful to their commercial enterprises. England's Loughborough University, for example, offers a Bachelor of Science degree in "Retail Automotive Management"—the country's first university-level degree in car-selling. Funding for the program is being provided in part by the Ford Motor Company.[19]

Since corporations need a steady supply of MBAs, business schools have little trouble attracting corporate support. In *Leasing the Ivory Tower*, Lawrence Soley describes how the funding sources for a new building at Michigan State's business school are documented in the names of various building components:

> "*The second floor of the building is named after the Kresge Foundation, a 350-seat lecture hall is named for the Ford Motor Company, the fourth floor is named for a Toyota dealer, the fifth floor is named for the Chrysler Corporation, and the MBA lounge is named for the First of Michigan Corp.*"[20]

Corporate labels go on more than just building parts. Thanks to Bank of America's $2 million donation to the University of California at Berkeley, the official title of the dean of the University's business school is "BankAmerica Dean".[21]

Though their influence is not always this visible, corporations are quite clear about what they expect from the educational system. In Britain, a Graduate Employability Test, which "objectively measures and profiles the skills most often specified by employers", focuses on just three areas: "business awareness", "personal working style", and "computer skills".[22] There is nothing location-specific about these skills, nor is there anything remotely connected with critical thinking, civic responsibility, or moral understanding.

Implanting Ideology

Corporations today "generously" offer teachers free study guides, magazines, posters, and other products for classroom use. As educational
materials their value may be dubious, but as vehicles for corporate
messaging, they are quite effective. Kellogg's produces "nutrition" posters that feature the company's cereals; the Hershey Food Corporation
distributes a video on geography, nutrition and science prominently
featuring Hershey's chocolate; Nike hands out free book covers plas-
tered with its logo. Today, virtually every Fortune 500 company has a
school project of a similar nature.[23]

Several companies have found a lucrative niche creating these
classroom materials. Often the goal is simply to familiarize impres-
sionable children with commercial products—as when third graders
learn to solve arithmetic problems by counting Tootsie Rolls, or
learn to read using the corporate logos of Kmart, Coke, Pepsi, or
Cap'n Crunch.[24]

Other times, more sophisticated ideas are implanted. Procter and
Gamble's teaching aid about labor issues, "Coping with Growth", essentially encourages children to accept corporate rule as a benevolent part
of the social order. A role-playing game within the curriculum asks
students to see events from the point of view of corporate management
during a series of strikes against the company in 1886:

> "Whenever the employees start a walkout you feel there ought
> to be some way of kindling among the workers a stronger feel-
> ing of respect for and loyalty to [the company].... How can they
> be convinced that their overall interests are truly inseparable
> from those of Procter and Gamble?"[25]

According to Michael Jacobson and Laurie Ann Mazur, authors of
Marketing Madness, similar materials have been created for industry
public relations arms ranging from the American Nuclear Society to the
National Frozen Pizza Institute. They also point out that the companies
producing these materials are clear about their purpose when solicit-
ing business:

"Let Lifetime Learning Systems bring your message to the classroom, where young people are forming attitudes that will last a lifetime," purrs the company's sales kit. "Whatever your objective, we can help you meet it.... Coming from school... all these materials carry an extra measure of credibility that gives your message added weight." Another ad asks potential clients to "IMAGINE millions of students discussing your product in class. IMAGINE their teachers presenting your organization's point of view."[26]

Not even pre-schoolers are safe from this corporate assault. Lifetime Learning Systems notes that by age four children are making "brand decisions", and—in an unintentionally profound statement—points out that "Preschool prepares children to become consumers".[27]

Educating children for roles in the corporate economy, indoctrinating them with an industrial worldview and an uncritical faith in technology, subjecting them to corporate manipulation in the classroom—all these are considered reasonable functions of the educational system. But even the fairly mild environmental programs underway in many schools have come under attack from an industry-led backlash. Turning reality on its head, critics claim that "unlike most schooling from kindergarten through 12th grade, environmental education often expressly encourages students to change their own behavior and that of their society."[28]

Re-localizing Education

Educational systems can still be redirected to serve the needs of communities rather than corporations and to enable individuals to participate in diversified local economies rather than becoming specialized, blinkered cogs in a global economy. What this would require is more educational diversity—systems of schooling that reflect local circumstances and teach ways of using nearby resources to meet local needs. This does not imply that the flow of information from other cultures should be shut off; in fact, an emphasis on local adaptation would give students a positive framework for understanding and respecting cultural differences.

Some shifts in the educational system could be fairly straight-forward. Direct experience of nature could replace much of the learning that now comes from books, videos, and computers. Some of this knowledge might be imparted better by parents and neighbors with an intimate knowledge of the local ecosystem than by formally-trained teachers. Food for school lunches could be provided by local farmers—and students could even grow some of their own—thereby providing a vital link to local resources and the local economy.

Rather than segregate children into factory-like same-age class-rooms that inherently foster competitiveness, a return to mixed-age classrooms—similar to the neighborhood one-room school houses that were once common in rural areas—would be a great improvement. Experience has shown that when children are in a position to help younger students and learn from older ones, cooperation rather than competition becomes the norm.

Apprenticeships in agriculture, forestry, and other means of local production should also be accorded their due as real and valuable forms of education. Such a shift would not only return children to their traditional place as important members of the local economy but would also impart a sense of responsibility to children at an early age.

These and many other changes would be beneficial. But since education currently perpetuates a broken form of society, it would be naive to think that fundamental changes in education will occur without a deep reordering of overall societal priorities. John Taylor Gatto, referring to American schooling in particular, argues that modern education does not allow children to grow into fully responsible, self-reliant adults, nor does it allow for their diversity:

> "As our economy is rationalized into automaticity and globaliza-tion, it becomes more and more a set of interlocking subsystems coordinated centrally by mathematical formulae which cannot accommodate different ways of thinking and knowing. Our profitable system demands radically incomplete customers and workers to make it go.[29]

"To rehumanize schooling", he adds, "we would need to re-humanize the economy and abandon our dreams of empire."[30]

June 30, 1996

GROOMED TO CONSUME
Anja Lyngbaek

Household consumption hits its yearly peak in many countries as the Christmas holidays approach. Despite homely pictures of tranquility on mass-produced greeting cards, Christmas has become more about frenzied shopping and overspending than peace on earth or quality time with family and friends. As with so much of our lives, the holidays have been hijacked by the idea that satisfaction, even happiness, is only one more purchase away.

Two generations ago, my Norwegian grandmother was overjoyed as a child when she received one modest gift and tasted an imported orange at Christmastime. In the modern era of long-distance trade and excess consumption, nobody gets even mildly excited by tasting a foreign fruit or receiving a small gift. Instead, adults dive into a cornucopia of global food (typically followed by a period of dieting) while children expect numerous expensive gifts—with designer clothes and electronic toys, games, and gadgets topping the list.

This comparison is not meant to romanticize the past or demean the present; it's just a small example of how consumption has come to replace the things that give real meaning to our lives—like creating something with our own hands, or sharing and interacting with others. In the process, we have been robbed of the ability to take pleasure from small wonders.

Most of us are aware that excessive consumption is a prime feature of modern life and that it is the cause of multiple social and environmental problems. We are living in what some call a "consumer culture"—a rather fancy title for something that has more in common with an abusive affliction, like bulimia or alcoholism, than it does with real living culture.

Rampant consumerism doesn't happen by itself: it is encouraged by an economic system that requires perpetual economic growth. When national economies show signs of slowing down, citizens are invariably called upon to increase their consumption, which in a country like the US represents 70 percent of GDP. Curiously, when talk turns to the downside of consumerism—resource depletion, pollution, or shoppers trampled at Walmart—it is the greed supposedly inherent in human nature that gets the blame. Rather than look at the role of corporate media, advertising, and other systemic causes of overconsumption, we are encouraged to keep shopping—but to do so "responsibly", perhaps by engaging in "green consumerism", a galling oxymoron.

I have no doubt that consumerism is linked with greed—greed for the latest model of computer, smartphone, clothes or car—but this has nothing to do with human nature. This sort of greed is an artificially induced condition. From early childhood our eyes, ears and minds have been flooded with images and messages that undermine our identity and self-esteem, create unnecessary wants, and teach us to seek satisfaction and approval through the consumer choices we make.

In fact, we are "groomed to consume". In the US, this means that the average young person is exposed to more than 3,000 ads per day on television, the internet, billboards and in magazines, according to the American Academy of Pediatrics.[1] While the figure may be lower in other countries, people everywhere are increasingly exposed to advertising—particularly through the internet. In fact, half of the global "consumer-class" can now be found in the "developing" world. Although per capita consumption in China and India remains substantially less than in Europe, those two countries now consume more in total than all of Western Europe.[2]

Marketing strategies—advertising, celebrity trend-setting, product placement in movies and TV shows, tie-ins between media and fast food franchises, etc.—have evolved to target an ever younger audience. According to sociologist Juliet Schor, media is even being created to target one-year olds. In Schor's book, *Born to Buy,* she defines "age compression" as the marketing to children of products that were previously designed for adults.[3] Examples include makeup for young girls, violent toys for small boys, and designer clothes for the first grader. Schor's research shows that the more children are exposed to media and advertising, the more consumerist they become; it also shows that they are more likely to become depressed, anxious and develop low self-esteem in the process.

However, children can become victims of the corporate-induced consumer culture even without direct exposure to advertising and media—as I learned during a year spent in my native Denmark, together with my then 12-year old son. Prior to our stay in Denmark, we lived in rural Mexico with limited exposure to TV, internet and advertising, surrounded by children from homes with dirt floors, wearing hand-me-down clothes. The need for designer wear and electronic gadgets had therefore never entered my son's mind.

However, after a few months of trying to fit in with Danish children, he became a victim of fashion, exchanging his usual trousers for the trend of the time—narrow sleek pants with diaper bottoms that impeded proper movement. Soon, style alone wasn't enough: the right brand name of clothes was added to his list of things required for happiness.

This same process was repeated in other parts of life. In Mexico, play would consist of an array of invented games, but a month in Denmark was sufficient for my son to feel too ashamed to invite anyone home because he didn't own an Xbox. During that year, he cried bitter tears over the absence of things that he had never thought he needed before: video games, Samsung galaxies, iPads and notebooks.

This rapid conversion of a unique individual into a global consumer wasn't a direct result of advertising but of the indirect influence of corporations on our minds and lives. The other children were as much victims as my own child, having to a large extent been robbed of the possibility to develop their own (corporate-free) identity and the imagination and creativity that comes with childhood.

Shifting away from a model based on ever-increasing consumption is long overdue. On a personal level, we can take positive steps by disengaging from the consumer culture as much as possible, focusing instead on activities that bring true satisfaction—like face-to-face interaction, engaging in community and spending time in nature.

In our very small rural community in Mexico, we have tried to do just that in our daily lives. Christmas for us is a communal celebration lasting several days, which includes music, dancing, playing (both indoors and outdoors) and cooking and baking lots of homegrown foods. A major part of the celebration is a gift exchange that celebrates our skills and creative powers. Rather than buying a multitude of gifts, we make one gift each to give to another person. Who we give to is decided in advance in a secret draw of names, not revealed until the exchange. For a month in advance, our community is buzzing with creative energy, as everybody—children and adults alike—is busy planning and making amazing gifts. Presenting our gift is the highlight of our celebration, even for the youngest. Thus, the coin has been flipped from consumption to creation and from receiving to giving.

However, while personal changes like this matter, they are not enough to turn the tide: structural changes are also required.

Despite dwindling natural resources, increasing levels of pollution and CO_2 emissions, and the many social costs of consumerism, no nation-state has yet been willing to renounce the economic growth model. This will not change until people pressure their governments to disengage from the current structure and to put the brakes on corporate control. This may sound undoable, but the existing system is man-made and therefore can be unmade. The trade treaties and agreements that favor corporations over nations, global over local, and profit over people and planet, can be revoked and transformed. All it may take is an alliance of a few strategic countries willing to say "STOP" to start a movement of nations willing to reclaim their economies.

When Jorge Mario Bergoglio was ordained Pope Francis, he came out with a public critique of the prevailing economic system that still rings true:

> "Some people continue to defend trickle-down theories which assume that economic growth, encouraged by a free market, will inevitably succeed in bringing about greater justice and inclusiveness in the world… This opinion, which has never been confirmed by the facts, expresses a crude and naïve trust in the goodness of those wielding economic power and in the sacralized workings of the prevailing economic system."[4]

Yet the blind belief in the economic growth model is waning as ever more people realize that the present economic model is playing havoc with people and planet. Even the strongest proponents of the current system are finding it harder to repeat the "more economic growth is the solution" mantra.

So let's downscale consumption this Christmas and celebrate creativity, community and our shared home—planet earth. Rather than commit to dieting in the new year, let's commit to joining the call for systemic change—away from a destructive global casino economy that concentrates power and wealth, towards place-based economies operating under democratic control and within ecological limits, with global wellbeing in mind.

January 2, 2014

OUR OBSOLESCENT ECONOMY
Steven Gorelick

A friend of mine from India tells a story about driving an old Volkswagen beetle from California to Virginia during his first year in the United States. In a freak ice storm in Texas, he skidded off the road, leaving his car with a cracked windshield and badly dented doors and fenders. When he reached Virginia he took the car to a body shop for a repair estimate. The proprietor took one look at it and said, "it's totaled." My Indian friend was bewildered: "How can it be totaled? I just drove it from Texas!"

My friend's confusion was understandable. While "totaled" sounds like a mechanical term, it's actually an economic one. If the cost of repairs is more than the car will be worth afterwards, the only economically "rational" choice is to drive it to the junkyard and buy another one.

In the "throwaway societies" of the industrialized world, this is an increasingly common scenario: the cost of repairing faulty stereos, appliances, power tools, and high-tech devices often exceeds the price of buying new. Among the long-term results are growing piles of e-waste, overflowing landfills, and the squandering of resources and energy. It's one reason that the average American generates over 70% more solid waste today than in 1960.[1] And e-waste—the most toxic component of household detritus—is growing almost 7 times faster than other forms of waste. Despite recycling efforts, an estimated 140 million cell phones—containing $60 million worth of precious metals and a host of toxic materials—are dumped in US landfills annually.[2]

Along with these environmental costs, there are also economic impacts. Not so long ago, most American towns had shoe repair businesses, jewelers who fixed watches and clocks, tailors who mended and altered clothes, and "fixit" businesses that refurbished toasters, TVs, radios, and dozens of other household appliances. Today, most of these businesses are gone. "It's a dying trade," said the owner of a New Hampshire appliance repair shop. "Lower-end appliances which you can buy for $200 to $300 are basically throwaway appliances."[3] The story is similar for other repair trades: in the 1940s, for example, the US was home to about 60,000 shoe repair businesses, a number that has dwindled to less than one-tenth as many today.[4]

One reason for this trend is globalization. Corporations have relocated their manufacturing operations to low-wage countries, making goods artificially cheap when sold in higher-wage countries. When those goods need to be repaired, they can't be sent back to China or Bangladesh—they have to be fixed where wages are higher, and repairs are therefore more expensive. My friend was confused about the status of his car because the opposite situation holds in India: labor is cheap and imported goods expensive, and no one would dream of junking a car that could be fixed.

It's tempting to write off the decline of repair in the West as collateral damage—just another unintended cost of globalization—but the evidence suggests that it's actually an *intended* consequence. To see why, it's helpful to look at the particular needs of capital in the global growth economy—needs that led to the creation of the consumer culture just over a century ago.

When the first Model T rolled off Henry Ford's assembly line in 1910, industrialists understood that Ford's technique could be applied not just to cars but to almost any manufactured good, making mass production possible on a previously unimaginable scale. The profit potential was almost limitless, but there was a catch: there was no point producing millions of items—no matter how cheaply—if there weren't enough buyers for them. And in the early part of the 20th century, the majority of the population—working class, rural, and diverse—had little disposable income, a wide range of tastes, and values that stressed frugality and self-reliance. The market for manufactured goods was largely limited to the middle and upper classes, groups too small to absorb the output of full throttle mass production.

Advertising was the first means by which industry sought to scale up consumption to match the tremendous leaps in production. Although simple advertisements had been around for generations, they were hardly more sophisticated than classified ads today. Borrowing from the insights of Freud, the new advertising focused less on the product itself and instead on the vanity and insecurities of potential customers. As historian Stuart Ewen points out, advertising helped to replace long-standing American values stressing thrift with new norms based on conspicuous consumption. Advertising, now national in scope, also helped to erase regional and ethnic differences among America's diverse local populations, thereby imposing mass tastes suited to mass production. Ewen notes that through increasingly sophisticated and effective marketing techniques, "excessiveness replaced thrift as a social value", and entire populations were invested with "a psychic desire to consume."[5]

Thus, the modern consumer culture was born not as a response to innate human greed or customer demand but to meet the needs of industrial capital.

During the Great Depression, consumption failed to keep pace with production. In a vicious circle, overproduction led to idled factories, workers lost their jobs, and demand for factory output fell further. In this crisis of capitalism, not even clever advertising could stimulate consumption sufficiently to break the cycle.

In 1932, a novel solution was advanced by a real estate broker name Bernard London. His pamphlet, "Ending the Depression through Planned Obsolescence", applauded the consumerist attitudes that advertising created during the 1920s, a time when "the American people did not wait until the last possible bit of use had been extracted from every commodity. They replaced old articles with new for reasons of fashion and up-to-dateness. They gave up old homes and old automobiles long before they were worn out."[6]

In order to circumvent the values of thrift and frugality that had resurfaced during the Depression, London argued that the government should "chart the obsolescence of capital and consumption goods at the time of their production... After the allotted time had expired, these things would be legally 'dead' and would be controlled by the duly appointed governmental agency and destroyed."[7] The need to replace these "dead" products would ensure that demand would forever remain high, and that the public—no matter how thrifty or satisfied with their material lot—would continue to consume.

London's ideas did not catch on immediately, and the Depression eventually ended when the idle factories were converted to munitions and armaments production for World War II. But the concept of planned obsolescence did not go away. After the War, its biggest champion was industrial designer Brooks Stevens, who saw it not as a government program but as an integral feature of design and marketing. "Unlike the European approach of the past where they tried to make the very best product and make it last forever," he said, "the approach in America is one of making the American consumer unhappy with the product he has enjoyed the use of…, and [making him want to] obtain the newest product with the newest possible look."[8]

Brooks's strategy was embraced throughout the corporate world and is still in force today. Coupled with advertising aimed at making consumers feel inadequate and insecure if they don't have the latest products or currently fashionable clothes, the riddle of matching consumption to ever-increasing production was solved.

The constant replacement of otherwise serviceable goods for no other reason than "up-to-dateness" is most evident in the garment industry, tellingly known as the "fashion" industry. Thanks to a constant barrage of media and advertising messages, even young children fear being ostracized if they wear clothes that aren't "cool" enough. Women in particular have been made to feel that they will be undervalued if their clothes aren't sufficiently trendy.

It's not just advertising that transmits these messages. One of the storylines in an episode of the 90s sit-com "Seinfeld", for example, involves a woman who commits the faux pas of wearing the same dress on several occasions, making her the object of much canned laughter.[9]

Obsolescence has been a particularly powerful force in the tech industry, where the limited lifespan of digital devices is more often the result of "innovation" than malfunction. With computing power doubling every 18 months for several decades (a phenomenon so reliable it is known as Moore's Law), digital products quickly become obsolete: as one tech writer put it, "in two years your new smartphone could be little more than a paperweight."[10] With marketers bombarding the public with ads claiming that *this* generation of smartphone is the ultimate in speed and functionality, the typical cell phone user purchases a new phone every 21 months.[11] Needless to say, this is great for the bottom line of high-tech businesses but terrible for the environment.

Innovation may be the primary means by which devices are made obsolete, but manufacturers are not above using other methods. Apple, for example, intentionally makes its products difficult to repair except by Apple itself, in part by refusing to provide repair information about its products. Since the cost of in-house repair often approaches the cost of a new product, Apple is assured of a healthy stream of revenue no matter what the customer decides to do. Indeed, iPhone 6 users who chose to have their device repaired at unauthorized (and less expensive) repair shops found that Apple had programmed the phones to cease functioning—known as being "bricked"—upon the unauthorized repair. "They never disclosed that your phone could be bricked after basic repairs," said a lawyer for the complainants. "Apple was going to... force all its consumers to buy new products simply because they went to a repair shop." [12]

In response to this corporate skulduggery, a number of states have tried to pass "fair repair" laws that would help independent repair shops get the parts and diagnostic tools they need, as well as schematics of how the devices are put together. One such law has already been passed in Massachusetts to facilitate independent car repair, and farmers in Nebraska are working to pass a similar law for farm equipment. But except for the Massachusetts law, heavy lobbying from manufacturers—from Apple and IBM to farm equipment giant John Deere—has so far stymied the passage of right-to-repair laws. [13]

From the grassroots, another response has been the rise of non-profit "repair cafés". The first was organized in Amsterdam in 2009, and today there are more than 1,300 worldwide, each with tools and materials to help people repair clothes, furniture, electrical appliances, bicycles, crockery, toys, and more—along with skilled volunteers who can provide help if needed. [14] These local initiatives not only strengthen the values of thrift and self-reliance intentionally eroded by consumerism, they help connect people to their community, scale back the use of scarce resources and energy, and reduce the amount of toxic materials dumped in landfills.

At a more systemic level, there's an urgent need to rein in corporate power by re-regulating trade and finance. Deregulatory "free trade" treaties have given corporations the ability to locate their operations anywhere in the world, contributing to the skewed pricing that makes it cheaper to buy new products than to repair older ones. These treaties also make it easier for corporations to penetrate not just the economies of the Global South, but the psyches of their populations—helping to turn billions more self-reliant people into insecure consumers greedy for the standardized, mass-produced goods of corporate industry. The spread of the consumer culture may help global capital meet its need for endless growth, but it will surely destroy the biosphere: our planet cannot possibly sustain more than 7 billion people consuming at the insane rate we do in the "developed" world—and yet that goal is implicit in the logic of the global economy.

We also need to oppose—with words and deeds—the forces of consumerism in our own communities. The global consumer culture is not only the engine of climate change, species die-off, ocean dead zones, and many other assaults on the biosphere, it is also hollowing out our communities, and even our own sense of self.

July 12, 2017

THE GLOBAL ECONOMY'S "IMPECCABLE LOGIC"

Steven Gorelick

Ever since the Occupy movement began using the term "the 1%" to signify the pinnacle of wealth and power, the gap between rich and poor has received a lot of attention. In his highly-regarded 2014 book, *Capital in the Twenty-first Century*, for example, Thomas Piketty's central thesis is that wealth inequality is bound to increase in modern capitalist economies.[1] This has been underscored by a series of Oxfam reports telling us that the inequality is even worse than we can imagine: that in 2019 the world's richest 1% had twice as much wealth as the world's poorest 4.6 billion; that by 2021 the 252 richest men had more wealth than all 1 billion women and girls in Africa, Latin America and the Caribbean combined; that the incomes of 99% of humanity declined during the Covid pandemic, even as the wealth of the world's 10 richest men doubled.[2] There's more, but you get the idea.

Statistics like these have led to widespread questioning of the moral underpinnings of the global economy. But does morality have any place in conventional economic thinking? While the overseers of the global economy are beginning to see problems with the wealth gap, it's for reasons that are neither moral nor ethical, but purely practical: extreme inequality, they fear, might threaten the continuance of the system itself. Christine Lagarde, Managing Director of the IMF, worries that "excessive inequality is not good for sustainable [sic] growth".[3] Meanwhile, billionaire and self-described plutocrat Nick Hanauer is even more concerned: "if we don't do something to fix the glaring inequities in our society, the pitchforks will come for us."[4]

To suggest that conventional economic thinking lacks a moral foundation is not to say that corporate CEOs and IMF economists have no moral or ethical values: most of them probably contribute to charity, feel tender thoughts towards their children and parents, and may even be angered at certain forms of injustice. The question instead is whether conventional economics regards wealth inequality as a moral, not just financial, issue.

To help answer that question, let's revisit a famous memo written by one of the most influential economists of our time, Lawrence Summers. The memo was written in 1991 when Summers was Chief Economist of The World Bank. In it he argues that heavily polluting "dirty industries" should be located in the less developed countries (LDCs). This is because the "cost" of illness and premature death is based on lost earnings, so the lives of the poor are less valuable than their wealthier counterparts: "From this point of view," Summers wrote,

"a given amount of health impairing pollution should be done in the country with the lowest cost, which will be the country with the lowest wages. I think the economic logic behind dumping a load of toxic waste in the lowest wage country is impeccable and we should face up to that."[5]

After arguing that "under-populated countries in Africa are vastly UNDER-polluted" and lamenting that high transportation costs "prevent world welfare enhancing trade in air pollution and waste," Summers concludes his memo with this:

"The problem with the arguments against all of these proposals for more pollution in LDCs (intrinsic rights to certain goods, moral reasons, social concerns... etc.) could be turned around and used more or less effectively against every Bank proposal for liberalization."[6]

In other words, any moral qualms about dumping toxic waste in poor people's backyards must be suppressed. Summers believes acknowledging the validity of those concerns would call into question the legitimacy of the entire "liberalization" package of deregulation and free trade pushed by The World Bank, IMF, WTO and other institutions. If moral values conflict with the economic model, Summers suggests, then those values must be abandoned.

One would expect that the leaking of this memo in 1992 would have irreparably damaged Summers' reputation and derailed his career. Indeed, there was outrage from certain quarters. Brazil's Secretary of the Environment, Jose Lutzenburger (an ardent environmentalist and winner of the Right Livelihood Award), wrote back to Summers: "Your reasoning is perfectly logical but totally insane... Your thoughts [provide] a concrete example of the unbelievable alienation, reductionist thinking, social ruthlessness and the arrogant ignorance of many conventional 'economists' concerning the nature of the world we live in.... If the World Bank keeps you as vice president it will lose all credibility." [7]

Not only did Summers hold on to his position at The World Bank, his career path continued ever upward. He was soon appointed to a number of high-ranking positions by President Bill Clinton, eventually rising to Secretary of the Treasury (where he presided over the deregulation of the financial industry); from 2001 to 2006 he served as President of Harvard University; after a stint as the managing partner of a major hedge fund, he was chosen by President Barack Obama in 2009 to head up his Council of Economic Advisers. [8]

There were some repercussions, however. Jose Lutzenberger was fired soon after writing his scathing criticism of Summers. [9]

Summers now claims that he signed the memo but didn't write it, that its contents were taken out of context, and that the whole thing was meant as sarcasm anyway. But the years that followed saw precisely the "welfare enhancing" trade in pollution that the memo called for. Dirty industries have, in fact, migrated to the less developed countries—accounting for both environmental improvements in the rich countries (about which Northerners are unduly proud) and horrifically blighted environments in places like China. Waste is now routinely traded to the Global South, with cargo ships bringing discarded plastic, e-waste, and other effluent of the consumer culture for disposal or "recycling", at great cost to their environment and the health of their citizens.

The "impeccable economic logic" which Summers embraced is deeply troubling, especially when so much of the global population is, by that logic, expendable: people who are admired in their communities, loved by neighbors, friends, and family; people who are caregivers for children and the elderly, who entertain and educate their communities as singers and storytellers; people who are honest and trustworthy, and serve as role models for the young. Such people may have countless admirable traits, but the only one that matters to mainstream economists is their contribution to global economic output. If in that arena—measured by their monetized earnings—they are deemed deficient, their worth becomes negligible. And as the wealth gap grows, millions more are joining the ranks of the expendable every year.

There will never be sufficient resources to bring all those billions of people up to the levels of income and consumption common in the west—something that even pie-in-the-sky economists who dream of endless "sustainable growth" must realize.

It's frightening to imagine what their next "welfare-enhancing" proposal will be.

March 19, 2015

THE SUPER BOWL OF SUBSIDIES
Kristen Steele

What comes to mind when you think of the Super Bowl? One team's stunning offense? The glitzy halftime show? Chicken wings and Clydesdales? Call me a spoil sport, but I can't help thinking *subsidies*. That's because even though the National Football League (NFL) generates about $2.8 billion a year in ticket sales, $2.3 billion in merchandising revenue, and an estimated $10 billion a year for television rights,[1] teams also receive massive subsidies to cover their capital costs. Between 1997 and 2015 alone, twenty new NFL stadiums were built with the help of $4.7 billion in taxpayer money.[2] Many teams also take a page from the playbook of the biggest global corporations by continually giving local governments ultimatums: unless taxpayers pony up for a new stadium or major improvements to the old one, the team will simply pack up and head elsewhere. What's even more galling is that until 2015, the NFL League Office even received a tax break because it was deemed a non-profit organization.[3]

I work for a very different scale non-profit for which all these millions and billions of dollars are impossible-to-fathom sums. However, the NFL's ability to fleece the public is nothing compared to most of the big—and even more dubious— subsidies out there. Local Futures tracks corporate subsidies, and these are some of the worst we've found:

Oil and gas
In 2016 the International Monetary Fund (IMF) estimated fossil fuel subsidies—including "externalized" environmental costs—for 191 countries. Among the biggest subsidizers were the US ($649 billion), China ($1.4 trillion), Russia ($551 billion) and the EU ($289 billion). Globally, the total comes to a $4.7 trillion for 2015 alone, and rising to $5.2 trillion by 2017—the equivalent of $10 million a minute.[4] While these figures include direct monetary gifts, tax exemptions, infrastructure and development support, price controls, and environmental costs, what it doesn't include is even scarier: it is conservatively estimated that world-

wide, there are 3.2 million premature deaths related to fossil-fuel air pollution every year—with some estimates putting the figure at nearly twice that number.[5] Other "externalities"—including environmental damage and the effects of climate change—defy quantification. The fact that none of these costs are included in the price of fossil fuels represents a huge hidden subsidy—big enough to make dubious ventures like tar sands extraction, to take just one example, seem economically viable.

Fishing

Despite severe declines in nearly every population of commercially-caught fish and calls for restrictions from scientists, politicians, and small fishers alike, industrial fleets are still given subsidies of about $35 billion per year.[6] Besides encouraging the unsustainable exploitation of dwindling species and condoning the ravaging of entire marine ecosystems, these subsidies directly undermine local, coastal economies. That's because the areas where small-scale fishermen were once able to catch enough for local markets have been scoured and fished out. Only the huge boats, with sonar-assisted fish tracking devices and nets big enough to swallow cathedrals, can chase after the remaining fish that have taken refuge far out at sea.

Agriculture

Among the WTO member countries, a reported $221 billion is given out in farm subsidies. When it comes to these kinds of hand-outs, much has been written about trade barriers, protectionism, price-fixing, and the poor farmers caught in the middle. The fact is that, for the most part, these subsidies neither hinder global trade nor keep small farmers solvent. In the US, two-thirds of the subsidies actually go to the wealthiest farms: "even celebrity hobby farmers such as Ted Turner, David Rockefeller, and Scottie Pippen collect subsidies that dwarf what the average family farmer receives."[7] Even more significant are indirect subsidies in the form of significant government aid for research and development (R&D) into biotechnology, new pesticides, and robotics that ends up supporting large-scale industrial agriculture and the agribusiness corporations that profit from it. Of the USDA's $3 billion R&D budget, less than 1% goes to organic agriculture.[8] You have to wonder how agricultural subsidies have been able to masquerade as support for farmers.

What all these subsidies have in common is that, without exception, they favor the big over the small, the global over the local and the polluting over the sustainable. Some call these "perverse subsidies" and there are, sadly, many more examples of them out there.

But it's important to recognize that these subsidies are *choices*: choices made by our leaders about how to spend our tax money. Whatever your opinion on taxation, the fact remains that most of us worked hard to earn those dollars. Should we not demand that they be used in ways that protect livelihoods, the environment, and our health?

You'll note that the industries that get the most subsidies also happen to be some of the most "profitable". Funny how that works. As with the tar sands example above, what would happen if we truly "leveled the playing field" and removed or shifted subsidies? Would small-scale wind power actually be more lucrative than fracking? Would fish rebound in coastal waters while everyone still got enough to eat? Would local food outcompete global food even on supermarket shelves? Based on numerous localization initiatives that are already tackling such issues around the world, the answer looks like a resounding yes.

To get back to my original topic, I know that many people, my dearly-loved brothers included, would probably be in favor of supporting the good ol' sport of football in this way. As one journalist wrote: "It's about the intangibles of identity and pride, which are far harder to value." I, for one, think that's a useful metric for more than just the NFL. Are we prouder of ravaged landscapes and emptied oceans than we are of clean air and waters full of life? Do we want to identify with a society that puts people and livelihoods first or one that idolizes corporate profits?

For me the answers are clear, and shifting subsidies is just about the simplest way to make our economies more ecologically-sound, more community- and people-friendly, and more localized. It is the goal—or touchdown, if you will—of economic localization.

September 18, 2013. Some statistics have been updated.

4

TECHNOLOGY VS. PEOPLE

PUTTING TECHNOLOGY
IN ITS PLACE
Helena Norberg-Hodge

A recent topic explored by the thinkers and activists who make up the Great Transition Network was "Technology and the Future". As writer after writer posted their thoughts, it was heartening to see that almost all recognize that technology cannot provide real solutions to the many crises we face. I was also happy that Professor William Robinson, author of a number of books on the global economy, highlighted the clear connection between computer technologies and the further entrenchment of globalization today.

As anyone who has followed my work will know, globalization is of particular interest to me. I've studied its impacts on different cultures and societies around the world—from Ladakh and Bhutan to Sweden and Australia—and a clear pattern has emerged: as people are pushed into deepening dependence on largescale, technological systems, ecological and social crises escalate.

I'm not the only one to have seen this. In the International Forum on Globalization—a network I co-founded in 1992—I worked with forty writers, journalists, academics and social and environmental leaders from around the world to inform the public about the ways in which "free-trade" treaties, the principal drivers of globalization, have eroded democracy, destroyed livelihoods, and accelerated resource extraction. In countries as disparate as Sweden and India, I have seen how globalization intensifies competition for jobs and resources, leading to dramatic social breakdown—including not only ethnic and religious conflict, but also depression, alcoholism and suicide.

Professor Robinson wrote that we are "at the brink of another round of restructuring and transformation based on a much more advanced digitalization of the entire global economy". This is true, but the link between globalization and technological expansion began well before the computer era. Large-scale, technological apparatuses can be understood as the arms and legs of centralized profit-making. And while

5G networks, satellites, mass data-harvesting, artificial intelligence and virtual reality will allow the colonization of still more physical, economic and mental space by multinational corporations, technologies like fossil fuels, global trading infrastructures, and television have already helped to impose a corporate-run consumer-based economy in almost every corner of the globe.

For reasons that are increasingly evident, an acceleration of this process is the last thing we need in a time of serious social and environmental crises. What's more, the technologies themselves—from the sensors to the satellites—all rely heavily on scarce resources, not least rare earth minerals. Some of the world's richest corporations are now racing each other to extract these minerals from the deepest seabeds and from the surface of Mars.[1] It has been estimated that the internet alone—with its largely invisible data warehouses (much of it manned by exploited labor in the "developing" world)—will use up a fifth of global electricity consumption by 2025.[2]

And for what? So that we can all spend more time immersed in and addicted to virtual worlds? So that we can automate agriculture, and drive more communities off the land into swelling urban slums? So that drones can deliver our online purchases without an iota of face-to-face contact?

When thinking about technology from within an already high-tech, urban context, we can easily forget that nearly half the global population still lives in villages, still connected to the land. This is not to say that their way of life is not under threat—far from it. Ladakh, the Himalayan region where I lived and worked for several decades, was unconnected to the outside world by even a road until the 1960s. But today you can find processed corporate food, smartphones, mountains of plastic waste, traffic jams and other signs of 'modernity' in the capital, Leh. The first steps on this path were taken in the mid-1970s when, in the name of 'development', massive resources went into building up the energy, communications and transport infrastructures needed to tie Ladakh to the global economy. Another step involved pulling Ladakhi children out of their villages into western-style schools, where they learned none of the place-based skills that supported Ladakh's culture for centuries, and instead were trained into the technological-modernist paradigm. Together, these forces are pushing the traditional way of life to the brink of extinction.

While that process began relatively recently in Ladakh, in the West it has been going on far longer, with deeper impacts. But even here, more and more people are becoming aware that the technologization of their personal lives has led to increasing stress, isolation, and mental health struggles. During the pandemic people have been forced to do more online than ever before—from classes to conversations with friends and family—and most have discovered how limited and empty online life can be. There is a clear cultural turning, visible now even in the mainstream, that goes beyond a desire to spend less time on screens. People are also beginning to reject the posturing of the consumer culture and its work-and-spend treadmill, wanting instead to slow down, to cultivate deeper relationships and to engage in more community-oriented and nature-based activities.

I see young people all over the world choosing to leave their screen-based jobs to become farmers. (This return to the land is happening in Ladakh, as well, which I find truly inspiring.) Informal networks of mutual aid are arising. Friends are gardening, cooking and baking bread together; families are choosing to live on the land and developing relationships with the animals and plants around them. We are seeing increased respect for indigenous wisdom, for women and for the feminine, and a growing appreciation for wild nature and for all things vernacular, handmade, artisanal and local. There is also an emergence of alternative, ecological practices in every discipline: from natural medicine to natural building, from eco-psychology to ecological agriculture. Although these disciplines have often been the target of corporate co-optation and greenwashing, they have invariably emerged from bottom-up efforts to restore a healthier relationship with the Earth.

All of these are positive, meaningful trends that have been largely ignored by the media, and given no support by policymakers. At the moment, they are running uphill in a system that favors corporate-led technological development at every turn. They testify to enduring goodwill, to a deep human desire for connection.

When viewed from a big-picture perspective, the expansion of digital technologies—which are inherently centraliz*ed* and centraliz*ing*—runs contrary to the emergence of a more humane, sustainable and genuinely *connected* future. Why should we accept an energy-and mineral-intensive technological infrastructure that is fundamentally about speeding life up, increasing our screen-time, automating our jobs, and tightening the grip of the 1%?

For a better future, we need to put technology back in its place, and favor democratically determined, diverse forms of development that are shaped by human and ecological priorities—not by the gimmicky-fetishes of a handful of billionaires.

January 3, 2022

RESISTING THE
TECHNOCRATIC PARADIGM
Steven Gorelick

E ver since the release of Pope Francis' encyclical, Laudato Si', people have been waxing rhapsodic about its message: finally, they say, a powerful global figure is explicitly calling for fundamental structural change.[1]

Unfortunately, the media has pigeon-holed the encyclical as a "climate change" document, so Francis's deep and broad critique of the modern economic system—with particular emphasis on its links to reductionist science and technology—isn't getting the attention it deserves.

This is not surprising. In America today, people are glued to screens and obsessed with their devices; they readily admit to being "internet addicts" and treat technology icons like Bill Gates and the late Steve Jobs as reverently as, well, the Pope. With media, advertising, and Wall Street continually whipping up enthusiasm for the next big thing, it is rare indeed to hear a fundamental questioning of the direction big business has taken science and technology. For this reason alone, it's worth looking at Francis' words in some detail.

Laudato Si' sets the stage with a Buddha-like acknowledgment— one that is repeated again and again—that "everything in the world is interconnected". The interconnectedness of all life is contrasted with a scientific paradigm based on reductionism—on eliminating or "controlling" outside influences so that bits of matter can be studied in isolation. While this approach has led to stunning technical advances, Francis points out that

"[t]he specialization which belongs to technology makes it difficult to see the larger picture. The fragmentation of knowledge ... often leads to a loss of appreciation for the whole, for the relationships between things, and for the broader horizon."

The knowledge that results, he says, "can actually become a form of ignorance."

We are now struggling to understand how Nature works and its importance, but also "every aspect of human and social life". A reductionist approach leads us to believe that the solution to insect pests is ever more powerful pesticides; that the solution to Islamist insurgencies is drone strikes against jihadist leaders; that the solution to virtually every societal ill is economic growth. A broad perspective makes it clear that all these "solutions" create more problems than they solve.

As Francis sees it, the reductionist worldview not only lies behind the many environmental crises we face, but it also constrains our response: "Technology... linked to business interests, is presented as the only way of solving these problems." This approach, he warns, is doomed to fail since it ignores the global system at the root of the problem: because the world is interconnected, we would fail to meet the climate, social, and economic challenges we are facing with tech and tech alone.

As Pope Francis notes, one particularly disastrous product of this fragmented worldview "is the idea of infinite or unlimited growth, which proves so attractive to economists, financiers and experts in technology. It is based on the lie that there is an infinite supply of the earth's goods, and this leads to the planet being squeezed dry beyond every limit."

Francis does not mince words when it comes to the disastrous marriage between a reductionist worldview and the corporate-led global economy. He states, "The alliance between the economy and technology ends up sidelining anything unrelated to its immediate interests. Consequently the most one can expect is superficial rhetoric, sporadic acts of philanthropy and perfunctory expressions of concern for the environment." These infrequent, disconnected acts will certainly not be enough to address the crises we face.

Additionally, Francis roundly rejects the argument that technologies are neither intrinsically good nor bad, and that it all depends on the uses to which they are put: "We have to accept that technological products are not neutral, for they create a framework which ends up conditioning lifestyles and shaping social possibilities along the lines dictated by the interests of certain powerful groups. Decisions which may seem purely instrumental are in reality decisions about the kind of society we want to build."

This is particularly so given the tremendous power of many new technologies, including nuclear energy, biotech, genetics, and data harvesting. Pope Francis notes that these new powers have given us "an impressive dominance over the whole of humanity and the entire world." Unfortunately, we can't expect that power to be used responsibly: "The economy accepts every advance in technology with a view to profit, without concern for its potentially negative impact on human beings."

One example of this is the impact on people and their livelihoods as human workers are increasing laid off and replaced with automated technology. For Francis, the unemployment that results is not only an economic problem, but a spiritual one: "Work is a necessity, part of the meaning of life on this earth, a path to growth, human development and personal fulfillment." Already, technology is creating more spiritual and economic issues than it is fixing.

Modern spiritual life is also weakened by consumerism, another arena in which technology and the global economy are closely entwined. The Pope notes, "a constant flood of new products coexists with a tedious monotony. Let us refuse to resign ourselves to this…. Otherwise we would simply legitimate the present situation and need new forms of escapism to help us endure the emptiness."

Francis is similarly concerned about the effects of digital media: "when media and the digital world become omnipresent, their influence can stop people from learning how to live wisely, to think deeply and to love generously…. they also shield us from direct contact with the pain, the fears and the joys of others and the complexity of their personal experiences." Aware, perhaps, of the many studies demonstrating a link between screen time and depression, he notes that media-dependence can lead to "a deep and melancholic dissatisfaction with interpersonal relations, or a harmful sense of isolation."

With the promises of technology proving hollow, "People no longer seem to believe in a happy future…. There is a growing awareness that scientific and technological progress cannot be equated with the progress of humanity and history, a growing sense that the way to a better future lies elsewhere." And yet voicing strong misgivings about technology is all but taboo in modern societies, as Pope Francis is well aware: "Whenever these questions are raised, some react by accusing others of irrationally attempting to stand in the way of progress and human development.... [But] a technological and economic development which does not leave in its wake a better world and an integrally higher quality of life cannot be considered progress. Frequently, in fact, people's quality of life actually diminishes."

What does Francis suggest we do?

In part, the solution involves seeing the technological worldview as one of the root causes of our current crises and working to resist it. We need, he says, "policies, an educational program, a lifestyle and a spirituality which together generate resistance to the assault of the technocratic paradigm."

Francis also believes that, rather than leaving decisions about technology to market forces, people must push for smaller-scale and less damaging technologies: "We have the freedom needed to limit and direct technology; we can put it at the service of another type of progress, one which is healthier, more human, more social, more integral." As an example, he cites small-scale, localized initiatives: "Liberation from the dominant technocratic paradigm does in fact happen sometimes, for example, when cooperatives of small producers adopt less polluting means of production, and opt for a non-consumerist model of life, recreation and community."

Despite the power of the techno-economic forces he critiques, Francis remains guardedly optimistic: "An authentic humanity, calling for a new synthesis, seems to dwell in the midst of our technological culture, almost unnoticed, like a mist seeping gently beneath a closed door." He questions whether the era of technological dominance can continue, "with all that is authentic rising up in stubborn resistance."

If the Pope continues to use his compassion, his intellect, and his moral authority in support of "all that is authentic", then the door to a new synthesis may yet swing wide open.

July 23, 2015

BRANDING TRADITION:
A BITTERSWEET TALE OF CORPORATE CAPITALISM
Steven Gorelick

I t's almost sugaring time here in Vermont. On our homestead we tap about 25 trees, boil down the sap on the kitchen cookstove, and, in a good year, end up with 4 or 5 gallons of maple syrup. That may sound like a lot, but since it represents our family's main source of sweetener, it's rarely enough to get us through the year. By mid-winter we're usually buying syrup from a neighbor—someone who makes his living from his sugar bush. His syrup comes in a gallon jug with an iconic sugaring image on the label—men in plaid jackets carrying sap buckets through the snow to a horse-drawn sled, the sugarhouse in the background nestled among the hardwoods, steam billowing from the cupola. One can easily imagine the age-old scene inside: neighbors trading jokes and gossip, eating homemade pickles, and dipping donuts into hot syrup, all accompanied by the roar of the fire and the hiss of the sap.

I had this image in mind as I read a disturbing news report about the industrialization of maple syrup production in Vermont. A company called Sweet Tree LLC (owned by a Connecticut-based investment firm) will soon be boiling sap from more than 100,000 taps in their gleaming new factory in Island Pond, a small town in the northeast corner of the state. If the company reaches its goal of 750,000 taps, it will be the largest sugaring operation in the world.

In the Sweet Tree factory, you won't find firewood gathered from the sugar bush: everything runs on electric power and fossil fuels. You won't find buckets, either: the sap is literally sucked out of the trees into pipelines using vacuum pumps, then passed through reverse-osmosis (RO) equipment to reduce its water content. There's no horse-drawn sled: the sap is delivered from the sugar bush to the factory in diesel tanker trucks. And neighbors won't be socializing in the sugarhouse: the door to this factory says, "Do Not Enter".

The forces transforming maple syrup production in Vermont are similar to those that have decimated small farms around the world. In both cases, the "technological treadmill" requires producers to make continual investments in equipment just to keep from falling behind—a race that small producers can't win. Most maple syrup producers abandoned sap buckets long ago for pipeline. Many use vacuum pumps to increase sap flow, and some use fossil fuels rather than firewood to boil it down. RO equipment, which shortens boiling time, is becoming increasingly common. All of these "advances" aim at increasing efficiency—shorthand for using technology and energy to reduce human labor. But the net effect is to increase the supply of maple syrup (thus keeping its price down) while requiring producers to pour tens or even hundreds of thousands of dollars into equipment. Smaller producers without the capital to invest or whose sugar bushes aren't big enough to justify the expense eventually give up. The same holds true for producers of milk, meat, vegetables, and anything else produced for national and global markets: if farmers can't get big, they have to get out.

Expensive labor-saving technologies not only make it difficult for small producers to survive, they also reduce the number of jobs available among those that remain. It's true that 24 jobs have been created in Island Pond by the Sweet Tree operation, but 100,000 taps divided among numerous small-scale operations would provide livelihoods for 5 to 10 times as many people. The local economic benefits would also be far greater: the profits from Sweet Tree's operation will be siphoned into investment portfolios in Connecticut, while the profits from those smaller producers would circulate locally.

The image on a gallon of maple syrup reflects a way of life—slower and less high-tech, more localized and neighborly—that many people rightly yearn for. Although Sweet Tree has no connection to that way of life, and in fact will help to undermine its remaining vestiges in Vermont, the company was drawn here because they can profit by associating their product with it. "We chose Vermont because it's pre-branded," said Sweet Tree CEO Bob Saul. "Thank you very much, state of Vermont, for having the best brand of any state."[1]

Can anything be done to stop the industrialization of maple syrup? One helpful step would be to give consumers a way to choose syrup that employs people rather than technology, uses less non-renewable energy, supports small farmers, and keeps money circulating locally. This could be done with a grading system based not on the color of the syrup (as is the case now) but on the level of technology employed in producing it. At one end of the spectrum would be operations that use sap buckets, human and animal power, and firewood gathered from the sugar bush. At the other end would be the syrup factory using pipeline, vacuum, RO, propane or fuel oil for boiling, and diesel trucks to haul the sap. Intermediate "grades" would reveal the extent to which energy-intensive, labor-destroying technologies have invaded the sugaring operation. Many people willingly pay more for food produced in ways that are better for the environment and small farmers, and there's reason to think the same would be true for maple syrup.

Here are some other suggestions:

- Small producers should be exempt from some of the government regulations that are currently applied to big and small producers alike—e.g. the requirement that every sugarhouse have an impermeable floor. Such rules can spell financial ruin for the smallest producers and are often unnecessary, especially when their products are sold locally.

- Publicly-funded research and development should focus on what small producers need, like inexpensive lead-free buckets, instead of working to develop newer and more expensive labor-displacing technologies. (The latest "revolutionary" advance from the University of Vermont's Proctor Maple Research Center involves planting maple saplings in dense rows, cutting their tops off, then vacuuming their sap into plastic bags!) [2]

- Schools, governments, and the media should stop denigrating manual labor. Farm and forest work—and physical labor in general—are systematically portrayed by these institutions as something to escape from; sitting in front of a computer, on the other hand, is consistently depicted as a high-status occupation. It's no wonder that so many children leave Vermont to seek employment while immigrant labor must be sought to fill the jobs on farms.

- Governments at all levels should put an end to the subsidies and tax credits that make technology and energy artificially cheap while making job creation artificially expensive. Without those supports industrial syrup production would not appear to be more "efficient", and traditional, labor-intensive syrup would actually be cheaper. Those same systemic supports are a major reason that small farms almost everywhere are being displaced by huge monocultural farms and feedlots, local businesses by big box stores, and factory workers by robots.
- Producers should be required to label their product with an image of their own sugarhouse, rather than an idealized image from 1920. Sweet Tree's label, for example, would show a 2-acre industrial metal-clad box.

Perhaps these proposals sound unrealistic at a time when country-of-origin labeling of meat has been struck down by the WTO and when GMO labeling (recently passed in Vermont) is being challenged in the courts by big agribusiness. But resistance to the further globalization and industrialization of food is imperative. If we passively accept the logic of industrial efficiency, there will be nothing left of small-scale farming but the nostalgic images on food packaging—branded images that are artificial, empty, and meaningless.

February 5, 2016

TECHNOLOGY AND ITS DISCONTENTS
Steven Gorelick

T ucked within the pages of the January issue of the *Agriview*, a monthly farm publication published by the State of Vermont, was a short survey from the Department of Public Service (DPS). Described as an aid to the Department in drafting their "Ten Year Telecom Plan", the survey contains eight questions, the first seven of which are simple multiple-choice queries about current internet and cell phone service at the respondent's farm. The final question caught my eye:

In what ways could your agriculture business be improved with better access to cell signal or higher speed internet service?

Two things are immediately revealed by this question: (a) The DPS believes that the only possible outcome from faster and better telecommunication access is that things will be "improved". (b) If you disagree with the DPS on point (a), they don't want to hear about it.

A cynic might conclude that the DPS is only looking for survey results that justify decisions they've already made, and that's probably true. But, more broadly, the department's upbeat, one-dimensional outlook on technological change is actually the accepted norm in America. In his book *In the Absence of the Sacred*, Jerry Mander points out that new technologies are usually introduced through "best-case scenarios". He notes: "The first waves of description are invariably optimistic, even utopian. This is because in capitalist societies early descriptions of new technologies come from their inventors and the people who stand to gain from their acceptance." [1]

Silicon Valley entrepreneurs have made an art of utopian hype. Microsoft founder Bill Gates, one of tech's most influential boosters, gave us such platitudes as "personal computers have become the most empowering tool we've ever created," [2] and, my favorite, "technology is unlocking the innate compassion we have for our fellow human beings."[3] Other prognosticators include Facebook founder Mark Zuckerberg, who informs us that social media is "making the world more transparent" and "giving everyone a voice."[4] Needless to say, Gates, Zuckerberg, and many others have become billionaires thanks to the public's embrace of the technologies they touted.

The DPS survey reveals another shortcoming in how we look at technology: we tend to evaluate technologies solely in terms of their usefulness to us personally. Jerry Mander put it this way: "[w]hen we use a computer we don't ask if computer technology makes nuclear annihilation more or less possible, or if corporate power is increased or decreased thereby. While watching television, we don't think about the impact upon the tens of millions of people around the world who are absorbing the same images at the same time, nor about how TV homogenizes minds and cultures... If we have criticisms of technology, they are usually confined to details of personal dissatisfaction."

The DPS survey demonstrates this narrow focus: it only asks how faster telecommunications will affect the respondent's "agriculture business", while broader impacts on family and community, on society as a whole and on the natural world are out of bounds. A narrow focus is especially problematic when it comes to digital technologies, because the benefits they offer us as individuals—ultra-fast communication, the ability to access entertainment and information from all over the world—are so obvious that they can blind us to broader and longer-term impacts.

Despite decades of hype and a continuing barrage of advertising, cracks are beginning to appear in the pro-digital consensus. The illusion that technology "unlocks compassion for our fellow human beings" has become harder to maintain in the face of what we now know: digital technologies are the basis for smart bombs, drone warfare, and autonomous weaponry; they enable governments to conduct surveillance on virtually everyone and allow corporations to gather and sell information about our habits and behavior; they permit online retailers to destroy brick-and-mortar businesses that are integral to healthy local economies.

We've also learned that social media doesn't just enable us to connect with family and friends, it also provides a powerful recruitment tool for extremist groups—from neo-Nazis and white supremacists to ISIS. And all but the most die-hard Trump supporters acknowledge that social media was used to disrupt the democratic process in 2016, and that it is effectively used by authoritarian political leaders all over the world, including Mr. Trump, to spread false information and "alternative facts".

People are even beginning to see that social media is not all that "empowering" for the individual. We recognize the addictive nature of internet use, though most of us don't yet take it seriously: a friend will say, "I'm totally addicted to Facebook!", and we'll just laugh. But it's not a laughing matter. According to *The American Journal of Psychiatry*, "Internet addiction is resistant to treatment, entails significant risks, and has high relapse rates." [5] The risks are highest among the young: a study of 14-24 year-olds in the UK found that social media "exacerbate children's and young people's body image worries, and worsen bullying, sleep problems and feelings of anxiety, depression and loneliness". [6] Not surprisingly, a 2017 study in the US found that the suicide rate among teenagers has risen in tandem with their ownership of smartphones. [7]

Little of this should have been surprising within the digital design world. Facebook's founding president, Sean Parker, now admits that the company knew from the start that they were creating an addictive product, one aimed at "exploiting a vulnerability in human psychology." [8] Nir Eyal, corporate consultant and author of *Hooked: How to Build Habit-Forming Products*, acknowledges that "the technologies we use have turned into compulsions, if not full-fledged addictions... just as their designers intended." [9]

These addictions have serious consequences not just for the individual, but for society as a whole: "The short-term, dopamine-driven feedback loops that we have created are destroying how society works. No civil discourse, no cooperation, misinformation, mistruth." This is not the opinion of some left-leaning Luddite, but Facebook's former vice-president for user growth, Chamath Palihapitiya. [10]

In these ways, digital technologies threaten the foundations of democracy. According to former Google strategist James Williams, "The dynamics of the attention economy are structurally set up to undermine the human will. If politics is an expression of our human will... then the attention economy is directly undermining the assumptions that democracy rests on."[11]

There is also evidence that a child's use of computers negatively affects their neurological development.[12] Tech insiders like Sean Parker may not know for certain "what it's doing to our children's brains," but Parker isn't taking any chances: "I can control my kids' decisions, which is that they're not allowed to use that shit."[13] Lots of other Silicon Valley technologists are keeping their children away from screens, in part by sending them to private schools that prohibit the use of smartphones, tablets, and laptops.[14] Meanwhile, the companies they work for continue to push their addictive products onto children worldwide: Alphabet, Google's parent corporation, provides "free" tablets to public elementary schools while Facebook recently launched a new app called Messenger Kids—aimed specifically at pre-teens.[15]

Much of the "best case scenario" for digital technology rests on its supposed environmental benefits (remember the "paperless society"?) But illusions about "clean" technology are dissolving in the horrific toxic wasteland of Boatou, China, where rare earth metals—needed for almost all digital devices—are mined and processed. Another dirty secret is the cumulative energy demand of all these technologies. It's estimated that within the next few years, internet-connected devices will consume more energy than aviation and shipping; by 2040, they will account for 14% of global greenhouse gas emissions—about the same proportion as the United States today.[16]

What does all this mean for ordinary citizens? For one, we need to begin looking beyond the immediate convenience that technologies offer us as individuals and consider their broader impacts on community, society, and nature. We should remain highly skeptical about the utopian claims of those who stand to profit from new technologies. And, perhaps most importantly, we need to allow our own children to grow up—as long as possible—in nature and community, rather than in a corporate-mediated technosphere of digital screens. Doing so will require us to challenge school boards and administrators who have been sold on the idea that putting elementary school children in front of screens is the best way to "prepare them for the future".

As for the Department of Public Service, my survey response will say that the costs of improved telecom access would far outweigh the benefits. It would be of no consequence to my farm business, which by design only involves direct sales to nearby shops and individuals. More importantly, our farm is not only an "agriculture business" it is also our home, and that's where the impact would be greatest. Better digital access would make it easier for me and members of my family to engage in addictive behavior, from online gambling and pornography to compulsive shopping, video games, and internet "connectivity" itself. It would consume the attention of my children, leaving them more vulnerable to insecurity and depression, while displacing time better spent in nature or in face-to-face encounters with friends and neighbors. There are broader impacts as well: we would be increasingly tempted to buy our needs online, thus hurting local businesses and draining money out of our local economy. And almost everything we might do online would add a further increment to the growing wealth and influence of a handful of corporations—Amazon, Google, Facebook, Apple, and others—that are already among the most powerful in the world.

These are significant impacts. But the DPS doesn't want to hear about them.

January 27, 2018

THE FOLLY OF FARM-FREE FOOD
Alex Jensen

"Beware of simple solutions to complex problems. That is a crucial lesson from history; a lesson that intelligent people in every age keep failing to learn"[1]

Having wisely counseled thus just five years ago in a trenchant critique of ecomodernism, environmental journalist George Monbiot's recent op-ed in *The Guardian* surprised a lot of people. In fact, one is left dizzyingly disoriented by Monbiot's recent change in opinion in which he promotes farm-free, "lab-grown food" using the very arguments he previously deconstructed and debunked when they issued from ecomodernist precincts.[2]

Monbiot and other cheerleaders for lab-grown food promote it as a quick way to arrest the juggernaut of industrial agriculture, skirting the messy and slow realm of politics.[3] Without question, industrial agriculture—and the globalized, industrial-corporate food system more broadly—is an unmitigated environmental and social disaster. In order to tackle climate chaos, soil loss, water depletion, biodiversity destruction, and much more, this system must come to an end, quickly. Yet, in promoting what Monbiot terms "farmfree food" as a solution to these crises, a key word from his analysis goes almost entirely and mysteriously missing: "industrial"

Proponents of lab food and other technological fixes fail to clarify that the many environmental problems they enumerate stem from large-scale, industrial agriculture and the globalized food system— whether of plant crops, animals, or their various entanglements.[4] They completely elide the hugely substantive differences between small-scale, diversified, agroecological and organic farming on the one hand, and large-scale industrialized agribusiness on the other. Instead, proponents cite controversial papers that argue, for example, in favor of confined animal feedlot operations (CAFOs) on the theory that they have lower greenhouse gas emissions vis-à-vis open grazing (the findings of which are at best debatable[5]), or that high-yielding agricultural systems generally have lower emissions than low-yielding ones.[6] Sadly, even though the latter study's authors have made it clear that they were not arguing that organic farming is necessarily low-yielding—and thus their paper shouldn't be seen as an endorsement of status quo industrial farming—this is exactly how it has been appropriated by chemical industry propagandists like the American Council on Science and Health (ACSH). This notorious anti-environmental front group[7]—which "defends fracking, BPA, and pesticides" and is funded by a rogue's gallery of corporate polluters—cited the same paper in an article with the provocative title, "Conventional Farms Are Better for Environment Than Organic Farms."[8]

Farmfree foodies as well as agribusiness hacks like the ACSH extrapolate from that study to conclude that the choice now is between intensification (meaning more production on existing farmland, usually through heavy inputs of chemicals) and extensification (assuming that eco-friendly farming necessarily is less productive and thus will need more land, in turn displacing wildlands). This is sometimes referred to as the "land-sparing vs. land-sharing" debate—a simplistic,[9] controversial, and far from settled[10] argument frequently deployed by industry apologists to greenwash agribusiness. A lot of the assumptions from the so-called land-sparing (i.e. intensive, industrial farming) side are questionable: for example the supposed universally low productivity of small/organic/agroecological farming; and the erroneous contention that intensification of existing farmland means wildlands will automatically be "spared".[11] Indeed, it is possible that these wildlands will be colonized by capitalist forces with chemical-intensive agriculture regardless (resulting in both. intensification and extensification) or destroyed and replaced by concrete, asphalt, subdivisions, et al. Monbiot's stance today in support of lab grown food not only ignores the flaws in these assumptions, it also runs counter to the arguments he made so well in his 2015 take-down of ecomodernism.

Regarding the impacts of agriculture on biodiversity—the destruction of which Monbiot is rightly panicked about—it is surprising that the lab-grown food crowd neglects research demonstrating the promise of interwoven "matrices" of highly productive, small-scale agroecological farms and biodiversity,[12] and the high compatibility of small-scale agroecology with biodiversity conservation. This research undermines his blunt generalization that "Every hectare of land used by farming is a hectare not used for wildlife and complex living systems."[13] He really means, every hectare of land used by industrial, chemical-intensive, monocultural farming is a hectare not used for wildlife and complex living systems.

The benefits of small-scale diversified agriculture are well-established, including that it's more productive per unit of land[14] and creates more livelihoods.[15] So, why are proponents of lab grown food embracing a narrow fix for our environmental crises while ignoring the burgeoning movements of agroecology, food sovereignty, permaculture, indigenous food systems, and so much else collectively comprising the worldwide local food movement? These latter solutions represent a florescence of initiatives that not only address ecological concerns, but also help heal the disastrous alienation of people from nature and from each other.

Promoters of lab food technology posit that even the best of farms, no matter how diversified, regenerative, and wildlife-friendly, represent a diminishment of the wild, a simplification of nature—an impact—that lab grown food can miraculously free us from. How? By ending farming and fishing and depositing fishers and farmers from nature into cities. In other words, lab grown food heralds an acceleration of urbanization. But does urbanization magically efface our impact on the living planet, does it spare the countryside and wildlands, releasing them for ecological relief and restoration? Hardly. This is a popular ecomodernist fantasy built on spurious and fanciful claims of the "dematerialization" and "weightlessness" of a future globalized, high-tech society.[16]

Eliminating farming and farmers, especially in the Global South where they still comprise majorities, and putting urbanization into hyper drive, would merely hasten the projected need for a doubling of the global building stock—that is, adding 2.48 trillion square feet (230 billion m²) of new floor area—by 2060, or "the equivalent of adding an entire New York City every month for 40 years."[17] All this new construction will mostly be of concrete, the "most destructive material on Earth", behind only coal, oil, and gas in carbon emissions and accounting for almost 1/10 of the world's industrial water use.[18] This spells ecological armageddon.

That "farmfree food" is also farmer-free food is not an insignificant matter in places where the majority of livelihoods are in small-scale farming. A conversion to lab grown food would lead to mass displacement of farmers. For those lucky enough to find other forms of employment, what would those be, exactly? Sedentary service sector jobs tied to consumerism? This is no environmental boon, no material "decoupling" of society from the planet, but rather a diffusion, externalization, and thus intensification of net impacts.

Worse, these efforts echo the prescription of those who would grab tribal and peasant agricultural lands for corporate or state-led industrialization in "fast-developing" countries around the world.[19] These projects also mimic the industrializing, anti-farmer prescriptions for agriculture that have afflicted much of the Global North.[20] Apart from their environmental impacts, land-grabbing, dispossession, and forced migration in search of work exacts devastating psychological, linguistic and other cultural losses in the process of estranging people from their traditional territories and lifeways. This is an anti-people and anti-environment agenda, and it's clear that those swooning over lab-grown foods and high-tech agriculture really haven't thought through the catastrophic and violent ramifications, especially for the still-farming majority in the Global South.

Urbanization is an environmental wreck for other reasons. For one, urban living produces more waste: "A city resident generates twice as much waste as their rural counterpart of the same affluence. If we account for the fact that urban citizens are usually richer, they generate four times as much."[21] Urbanization and its outsourced ecological footprints do not spare forests, either, but rather hasten their demise, according to science journalist David Biello:

> "a statistical analysis of 41 countries revealed that forest loss rates are most closely linked with urban population growth and agricultural exports from 2000 to 2005—even overall population growth was not as strong a driver .... In other words, the increasing urbanization of the developing world—as well as

an ongoing increase in consumption in the developed world for products that have an impact on forests, whether furniture, shoe leather or chicken fed on soy meal—is driving deforestation, rather than containing it, as populations leave rural areas to concentrate in booming cities."[22]

Similarly, research has shown that urbanized, affluent, consumerist countries are the primary threats to biodiversity "hotspots" around the world—threats linked to production for international trade.[23]

What about the mental health implications of pulling people off the land and into urban zones? Many countries today are beset by an epidemic of loneliness as well as increasing rates of depression, schizophrenia, and chronic stress—afflictions that are closely linked to competitive neoliberal economies and exacerbated by urban living.[24] Not surprisingly, research has shown that human psychological health is better-served by small-scale, rural, and community living.[25]

Community is a "potent cure" for mental illness and loneliness,[26] but the lab-grown food craze disregards the important role played by local food economies—which link local farmers, consumers, and institutions in mutually interdependent webs—in rebuilding communities torn asunder by the heartless advance of the global consumer culture. Community can be built in other ways besides local food systems, but the latter, based in substantive, material interdependency, are key to forging robust, durable, resilient bonds.

Moreover, gardening and small-scale farming—especially when done cooperatively in groups and in conditions of economic security (i.e., not the kind of highly exploitative conditions endured by many farmworkers on industrial farms)—are known to be good for physical and mental health precisely because of their relative lack of "labor-saving" devices. "Despite the popular prejudice," Robert Netting pointed out in his classic book *Smallholders, Householders*, "labor-saving is not the chief end of life, and farm work is not a bad thing."[27] These activities involve manual labor, bodily exertion and movement, expose us to microbes beneficial to health,[28] and enable us to connect to nature and other people.[29] By simply supplying people with factory-derived sustenance, lab grown food will rob us of this potential source of meaning and health.

An important factor underlying today's ecological crisis is our alienation from the natural world, which leads to our ignorance about and, thus, indifference towards its destruction.[30] We—and crucially, our children—need to play in and interact with the natural world, including through "fieldwork in the countryside."[31] The expanding technological sphere has already alienated us disastrously from the natural world. Deepening the technologization of agriculture through developments like lab grown food will hasten this separation in one of the last vocations where the rift could, with a shift towards small-scale agroecology, be repaired.

It's true that one can interact with the natural world in ways other than food production, and more and more research is revealing the powerful health and social benefits of spending even small amounts of time in natural areas.[32] Yet as Chris Smaje observes, "making people mere spectators of the natural world is unlikely to do either people or the natural world a long-term favor."[33] If the spectator-recreationist model of connecting with nature were sufficient, we should have already solved the ecological crisis based on national park visitation numbers alone. The fact that we haven't reveals the model's inability to materially alter our economies and ways of living. Wendell Berry argues that good stewardship of land and a healthy relationship with the rest of nature "turns on affection", and affection requires intimate, long-term, physical interaction with the land and the kind of dense ecological knowledge and wisdom that only such interaction produces. By obviating the need for hands on the land—or "eyes per acre" as Berry calls it— lab grown food is inimical to forging this affection and can only accelerate our alienation from and indifference to nature, to its detriment and ours.[34]

Dealing with these myriad consequences of a boom in lab grown food would not be a simple thing. Mass displacement of farmers and accelerated urbanization would have to be mitigated at a policy level, and the consolidation of corporate power within the lab grown food industry would have to be held firmly in check. Yet pessimism about governments' ability to properly regulate our food systems is why some people are giving up on the entire constellation of ecological farming possibilities in the first place and becoming attracted to techno-fixes. But will regulating lab grown food be any less messy, political, or slow than simply changing agriculture for the better?

Stepping back and looking at all these strands together, it seems clear that what we urgently need—for both environmental and social protection and well-being—is precisely the reversal of developments of the lab grown food ilk and political-economic support for the sustainable re-inhabitation of the countryside through localization and decentralization of our food systems. In the face of unemployment, the potential of small-scale, diversified, less-mechanized agriculture to generate jobs and livelihoods is considerable;[35] what's more it's necessary to effect a transformation toward a regenerative, fossil-fuel-free, agroecological future.[36] This is exactly what the international food sovereignty movement is calling for through networks like La Via Campesina, what so many young people are aspiring to through organizations like the National Young Farmers Coalition in the US and the Landworkers' Alliance in the UK, and what the local food movement is espousing all over the world. To support a "farm-free" future is to pull the rug out from these, some of the strongest allies in the struggle against corporate agribusiness and globalization.

Hopefully, sincere environmentalists who are attracted by the siren song of lab-grown food will take a hard look at the implications of a world without farmers and see that this techno-fix actually supports an industrial food system that is rotten to the core.

In addition to the work already happening at the grassroots, major policy changes will be required to radically transform the food system in ways that bridge the gap between humans and the land. This in turn will require massive pressure from below on policymakers who, for the most part, are servile to corporate power and under the sway of conventional economic assumptions.

This is not a "simple solution" to the complex problems of food and the environment. But in the long run it's probably the only real one.

March 1, 2020

5

TOWARDS NEW ECONOMIES

IN PRAISE OF SMALL SCALE
Helena Norberg-Hodge

Societies around the world face a mounting number of crises—from climate change and unemployment to rising levels of depression, inequality, extremist nationalism and more. If we see these problems as separate and distinct—each with its own unique causes and solutions—we can easily feel overwhelmed and hopeless. But these seemingly disparate crises are actually *linked*—they share a common root cause—and focusing on that root cause enables us to address our multiple social, as well as environmental problems, simultaneously.

My observations and studies throughout the world—from the least to the most industrialized regions—have convinced me that our many crises are the product of an economic system that is so large, so global that it has truly become an *invisible* hand. The global market is steering development towards resource- and energy-intensive jobless growth, creating fear, insecurity and pollution worldwide.

How did we end up in this situation? To answer that question, we need the bigger picture, the long view. The economic system of today has its roots in European conquest and colonialism. As the colonial powers expanded across the world, global traders gained immense power and wealth. Although the end of colonialism made it appear that the former colonies became independent, the dismantling of their once self-reliant local economies left them dependent upon—and subservient to—a trade-based global economy centered in the West. That dependence was intensified through "development" programs—mostly focusing on building up a trade-based infrastructure—that pushed newly-independent countries into indebtedness in which most remain mired.

Even in the North, subsidies, taxes and regulations have long favored the big and the global, while undercutting human-scale self-reliant economies. In the belief that bigger is better, governments have provided huge incentives to global players that are denied to smaller producers. This is why butter from New Zealand costs significantly less in the UK than butter from the farm down the road, and why Chinese businesses—seeking to benefit from the tax breaks given to globally-traded products—commonly export and then re-import the same goods.

Subsidies and tax breaks are not the only rules of the game that favor global players, Thanks to the "free trade" treaties by which governments have handed over increased freedom, wealth and power to giant multinationals, corporations can produce in countries where people earn a dollar a day, while selling in countries where people earn a hundred dollars a day. This process is destructive to people on both sides of the ledger, while benefiting only a relative handful of global banks and corporations.

Among the results is that the distance between production and consumption of even our most basic needs have been stretched to absurd lengths, as has the distance between people and power. As the scale of the economy grows, those who have the most influence over our future become increasingly distant: a corporate executive in a far-off city can decimate a thriving local economy by deciding to shift production to where labor is cheaper, or by marketing heavily subsidized, artificially cheap products that outcompete local production. Worst of all, deregulated global banks and financial institutions are free to make trillions of dollars out of thin air, imposing them as debt on individuals and whole nation states.

Such actions are not born of malice, but a narrow perspective that is endemic to large-scale, highly specialized economies: decisions are made on the basis of numbers on a page—corporate profits, share price, rates of GDP growth—not their broad, real-world impacts.

This is comparable to the situation faced by the typical shopper at a supermarket, who can find it virtually impossible to know much more than the price of the items on the shelf. Were farmworkers treated well and paid fairly, or were they abused? Were the ingredients grown sustainably, or in a chemical-drenched monoculture clearcut from old-growth rainforest? Even an "organic" label can be suspect when the product was grown and certified on the other side of the world.

But it would be unwise to blame the CEO or the supermarket shopper for the state of the world; both are working within a system that exports and conceals the impacts of our choices, disabling ethics and blinkering us to the big picture. Government subsidy and tax policies, meanwhile, usually reward choices that are destructive to people and the planet.

Reversing this situation requires reducing the power of unelected businesses and banks. This may seem an impossible task, but there is a glimmer of hope on the horizon. More and more people are waking up to the structural reasons why eight men own more than 3.5 billion people, why CO_2 emissions continue to escalate, and why our governments are listening to the sound of capital rather than the voices of their citizens. People are creating alliances that bridge once-divisive gaps—between social activists and environmentalists, between labor unions and small businesses, between North and South. These alliances have even become powerful enough to stall the trade agreements. It's important to keep in mind that opposition to these treaties has come from the grassroots, not from what the media describes as "populist" leaders.

Exposing the economic system as the root cause of so many of our crises brings with it enormous potential for healing, for moving beyond "them and us", left and right, or the politics of identity. It also goes beyond the maligning of human nature—the belief that the root problem is human greed, rather than a destructive global economic system that *creates* greed in order to spur consumption.

In our crisis-ridden modern world, it is high time that we fundamentally shift the skewed structures of the global economy and make way for something that makes a lot more sense: smaller scale. The good news is that changing the direction of the economy would be far easier than changing human beings or the trajectory of evolution.

What do human-scale economies actually look like? They look like the societies humans have lived in for most of our species' history. In those traditional cultures important resources (like rivers, pastures, forestland) were held in common, and others (like tools and implements) were often shared—as was labor, particularly during harvests and other busy times of the year.

Another common feature was a sense of interdependence, both between people and beyond the human community to the natural world: people in human-scale economies recognized that they are part of a much larger fabric of life.

Education in such cultures was location-specific: rather than learning a supposedly universal set of facts, children learned how to survive and thrive in a particular place. This meant understanding the resources at hand, the intricacies of local micro-climates, soils, and locally-adapted seed varieties and animal breeds.

These patterns are being rediscovered in the growing localization movement. By scaling down and localizing our economies, we not only minimize the drivers of our most vexing problems, we incorporate the healthier patterns typical of traditional cultures into our own way of life. The goal is not for all of us to become hunter-gatherers or self-reliant farmers, but to reduce both the scale of the economy and the distance between production and consumption—changes that bring the economy back home.

Local economies reverse the systemic forces that have done so much damage to farmers' livelihoods, the environment, and the quality of our food. As citizens become better educated about the realities of the global economy—recognizing both the hidden subsidies that make global food seem cheap as well as the hidden costs of inflated food miles—they are becoming more appreciative of local, seasonal foods. When enough of them pressure their political leaders to reverse the systemic supports that make global food cheaper than local food, the global food system will no longer stand.

In human-scale economies, the principle of diversity is not limited to food and farming, but extends to the full range of economic activity. Instead of one or two big hypermarkets on the outside of town dominating economic exchange, the high-street of each village or neighborhood becomes a bustling center for a variety of small shops and businesses to offer their goods and services, in turn providing a far greater number of job opportunities for local people.

Localizing education means that young people are no longer trained to fill increasingly specialized jobs in the corporate economy, but instead receive a variety of practical skills suited to life in their bioregion. In this way, we mirror the kinds of education offered in traditional cultures, where children learn to meet the needs of their community by maximizing the use of local resources and minimizing impacts on the environment. Importantly, the knowledge undergirding local self-reliance implies a deep awareness of limits. It is only by reifying an abstraction—money—that economists can believe in endless growth.

Perhaps most importantly, human scale economies reweave the fabric of connection to Nature and to one another by restoring a strong sense of interdependence. In this way, the localization movement is already proving itself a powerful antidote to both personal insecurities as well as societal ills, including ethnic, economic and intergenerational rifts.

This has already become apparent in those communities in the global North where people have chosen to abandon the fast-paced competitive consumer culture: residents find that life is far more pleasant when human-scale interdependence shapes social interactions.

Scaling down and localizing our economies does not mean retreating into isolationism or closing ourselves off to other cultures. In fact, we need international collaboration more than ever today—not only to combat and adapt to global environmental problems like climate change, but to create the cross-border alliances needed to counter the forces of globalization.

At the same time, we need to support and join local initiatives like ecovillages, consumer-producer co-operatives, farmers' markets, community gardens, local business alliances, local finance, time-banking, and community-supported agriculture. These efforts not only lessen our dependence on the global economic juggernaut, they are the building blocks of healthy, human-scale economies based on local interdependence. They are already building a better future for an increasing number of communities.

February 15, 2017

RESIST GLOBALLY, RENEW LOCALLY
Helena Norberg-Hodge

A recent discussion forum among the members of The Great Transition Network focused on "The Promise and Pitfalls of Localism." My friend and colleague Brian Tokar started the discussion by noting that even though there is a resurgence of progressive action at the local level, "reactionary nationalist movements in Europe and beyond seek to position themselves as the true voices of a renewed localism."

Both parts of Brian's observation are correct. But the fact that the language of localism is being increasingly co-opted by authoritarians around the world is itself a sign of localism's appeal. Left uprooted and adrift by the globalized economy, people are desperate for a sense of connection: to one another, to the living world, to a place and a culture that's familiar to them. Demagogues from Donald Trump to Marie Le Pen to Jair Bolsonaro have capitalized on this longing and turned it towards nationalistic and bigoted ends.

We cannot eliminate the natural human desire for rootedness. Instead, we need to make a very clear distinction between localism and nationalism.

For most of our time on this planet, we evolved in intergenerational communities, closely bonded to the land, to the plants, to the animals around us. Instead of being dependent on distant, anonymous institutions and businesses, we depended on one another in human-scale structures and institutions. Localism taps into this deep need for community and a sense of place.

Nationalism, on the other hand, destroyed our sense of interdependence with human-scale community and the living environment. Boundaries that ignored natural bioregional and cultural connections were forged by elites to create new artificial identities that promoted centralized power and, in many cases, the war machine.

To restore localized structures, we will need to enact a series of systemic changes to the way the global economy functions. Doing this would reduce or eliminate psychological as well as economic insecurity, and greatly lessen the appeal of authoritarian leaders, who prey on these insecurities and use them to their advantage.

The faux-localism of "us vs. them", I have found, only emerges after genuinely community-based localism has broken down: it is a pale shadow that can only thrive in the absence of the real thing. I spent decades of my life in Ladakh, India, and witnessed firsthand what happened when the region was opened up to the global economy. The economic base of society veered sharply from self-reliant agriculture to jobs in government and tourism. People were pulled away from decentralized villages into the capital. Buddhists and Muslims who had previously lived in an interdependent economy were now pitted against each other over scarce employment opportunities. At the same time, exposure to the Western consumer culture—mostly through advertising and tourism—led to feelings of cultural and individual inferiority. One of the results of this upheaval was the sudden emergence of tension, conflict, and eventually violence between Buddhists and Muslims—a situation which had never previously existed in Ladakh.

Physical dislocation, the breakdown of community, psychological as well as economic insecurity—all products of economic globalization—bred intolerance. These same factors are now causing similar problems around the world.

Because of this, what I call "big-picture activism" will be necessary to plant the seeds and tend the shoots of a genuinely liberatory and regenerative localism. We need to raise awareness about the fact that governments are subsidizing and deregulating multinationals, while punishing individuals and place-based businesses within the national arena with heavy taxes and onerous regulations. We need to pressure for changes in taxes, subsidies and regulations, in order to shift support from large and global businesses towards those small local and regional businesses that will form the bedrock of the economies of the future. At the same time, grassroots activism will be needed to help reconnect people with the communities from which they have become alienated, and to amplify the voices of indigenous peoples and others who have preserved the knowledge of how to live truly place-based lives.

Steps Towards Transformation

What I am building toward here is a two-pronged theory of change that I often describe with the words "resistance and renewal." It is at once "top-down" and "bottom-up." Resistance to corporate rule at the policy level will need to be coupled with the generation of alternatives from below, to fill the gaps left by the departing old system. This is not about ending global trade or industrial production; but for most of our needs, we will need to shift towards smaller scale and more localized structures: decentralized, community-controlled renewables for energy, revitalized local food systems to feed us, and robust local business environments to employ more people and keep wealth from draining out of our communities.

We can begin this process without national governments on our side. Indeed, it is unlikely that they will jump on this bandwagon before it has already become unstoppable. Instead, we should look to local governments for solidarity. Mayors and local councils are already realizing what higher levels of government have not: that economic and political self-determination go hand in hand.[1] Community rights ordinances, public banks, innovative local food purchasing programs—there are countless models showing how local governments can support local resilience.

The key to integrating efforts at resistance and renewal lies therefore in building a sense of civic engagement beyond the ballot box. Consumer culture would have us think of ourselves as discrete individuals driven by self-interest, with no allegiance to anything larger than ourselves. But countless initiatives that are rebuilding community connections and deeper relationships to the natural world are already proving effective in reducing depression, anxiety, friction and violence. And by revitalizing town squares and main streets and reinvigorating the public sphere, local empowerment gives the lie to the message of separation. We must leverage all the tools and passions of local activists, consumers, producers and local enterprises, to show what is possible when we act in solidarity with our neighbors. We must demonstrate that local economies work, and work well, and then build from there.

Scaling Sideways and Up

In his opener, Brian Tokar raised the question of whether locally based movements can effectively address problems that are global in nature. The one global problem that looms above all others is, of course, climate change, so it makes sense to ask what the program of economic localization I have just outlined can offer on that front. For one thing, the volume of global trade—which currently accounts for 4% of the world's carbon emissions and is set to rise to 17% by 2050 under current trade rules—would be curbed in an economically localized world. For another, moving from the industrialized, global food system to more localized, diversified food economies would not only allow soils to sequester carbon rather than eroding into the sea, it would also liberate us from the yoke of multinational corporations and massively reduce our dependence on plastic and fossil fuels. The creation of interdependent, local food economies would also mean that biodiversity—both wild and agricultural—would no longer be sacrificed on the altar of corporate profits. A further benefit is that both the scale and the impact of climate-driven migration would be blunted by the emergence of more resilient local economies across the global North and South. Even in the absence of formalized coordination among the world's localization movements, the whole would be—and in many places, already is—greater than the sum of its parts.

There are a number of networks of localist movements already in existence, from La Via Campesina and the Global Ecovillage Network to permaculture and the Transition Network. In these alliances, channels of cross-initiative communication are being opened up, not just for the purpose of information-sharing, but also for direct collaboration—and, in some cases, for the hashing-out of differences of opinion regarding future steps. We will have to bear in mind the lessons learned through the processes of engagement within these networks if we wish to scale the localization movement "sideways and up" in any coordinated fashion—for example, to tackle the climate crisis or trade policy at the level of international institutions.

In the meantime, the seeds of our local future continue to be planted every day. Local Futures has collected some of the most inspiring and successful examples in our Planet Local library. As the fault lines in the global economy continue to grow, and the desire for genuine human connection becomes ever more keenly felt, these existing initiatives will provide direction as well as inspiration, and stand as a compelling alternative to the faux-localist path of violence, fear, and hate.

August 15, 2019

WHAT TO DO
WHEN THE WORLD IS ON FIRE

Henry Coleman

I n December of 2019, my best friend Kit took me and my partner to the place where she grew up, in the remote Thora Valley, in
the pristine forested foothills of Eastern Australia's Great Dividing
Range. As we drove down Darkwood, the single road into the Thora,
Kit told us stories of floods and moldy houses, of Christmases spent
at swimming-holes and mushroom picking in the rain. She pointed to
where you'd usually be able to see the dramatic ridgelines of the Dorrigo
escarpment, one of Australia's last strongholds of primordial Gondwanan rainforest.

But in December 2019, the Dorrigo escarpment, along with the rest
of the country's south-east, was shrouded in the thick smoke of Australia's worst bushfire season on record. Rainforests were burning that had
never known flames before. 'Megafires' was suddenly a household term.

Never mind—we were in one of the wettest parts of the entire continent, adamant that there were still swims to be had, beauty to be enjoyed
and peace to be felt.

In the red-tinted afternoon light, we pulled over to ask an old farmer
the way to a campsite. He opened the gate to his riverside cow paddock
and invited us to pitch our tent there. I was touched that this kind of
generosity and trust between strangers still persists—once you get away
from the big cities, at least.

Despite the blackened leaves and long strips of charred bark that
rained down on us from the oppressive, bruise-yellow cloud of smoke
that filled the sky, we had a sweet time in that paddock—making dinner,
looking for platypus in the river and telling stories in the tent at dusk.

Then, our hearts skipped a beat. We watched through the flyscreen
as the faint orange glow on the horizon suddenly combusted, sending
a plume of magenta flames into the sky. We could hear the roar as the
blaze consumed the entire mountainside to the south-west in a matter
of seconds. Left with little choice, we hurriedly packed up our tents and

drove oceanward. I will not forget the overwhelming sense of hopeless-ness and utter inadequacy I felt as we said goodbye to the generous old farmer, who chose to stay and defend his home.

As a nature-lover and lifelong birdwatcher, that feeling echoed a greater despair. This planet and her kaleidoscope of species have given me so much—provided me so generously with food for the body, mind and spirit. And yet, in the face of anthropogenic climate change, can I do nothing but panic and watch her go up in flames in my rear-view mirror?

Unfortunately, this story does not pertain only to Australia. In 2020, Siberia, Indonesia, Brazil and Argentina all experienced their worst wildfires in decades, and as I write this the western USA is currently in the throes of an unprecedented inferno. My heart goes out to all those countless humans and non-humans who have lost their homes and their lives.

It also goes out to all the young people in the world who justifiably fear for their future. In 2018, the Intergovernmental Panel on Climate Change informed us that we have no more than twelve years left to limit climate change to avoid untold catastrophe. As young people, how can we possibly open ourselves up to this suggestion, while retaining enough hope to work for change? The new megafire reality now incites me and my partner to question our dreams of moving to the bush and building a little house—is it now a reckless decision to leave the concrete insula-tion the city affords, and live a life in Nature? For others, like the Thora Valley farmer (and the rest of the rural half of humanity), is it a reckless decision to stay in their homelands and maintain land-based ways of living? Should we all accept a destiny of total urbanization, turning our backs on a burning world in favor of the climate-controlled "smart city"?

Most global business leaders would not hesitate to answer an emphatic 'yes' to that question. After all, many of them expressly believe that our species is destined to dwell in the realm of robots, internet, spaceships and ultra-modern megapolises, and not in the realm of forests, small farms, koalas and riverine swimming holes. In the fantasies of Google's Ray Kurzweil, our food will come from "AI controlled vertical buildings" and include "in-vitro cloned meat".[1] In the not-so-humble opinion of Tesla's Elon Musk, building a city on Mars is "the critical thing for maximizing the life of humanity", even as Earth's cities will soon require "30 layers of tunnels" to relieve congestion.[2]

And it's not just the tech bros who paint this kind of future-vision. Much of the environmental movement is on board with it, too. In the crude belief that humanity needs to consume ever more energy, they are pushing "Green" policy packages and Corporate Social Responsibility programs that will plaster fertile soil with solar panels and pave mountaintops to accommodate wind turbines. Our governments are investing in huge, power-hungry technologies to suck carbon out of the atmosphere, while geo-engineers propose bleaching the stratosphere with sulphur dioxide to reflect infrared sunlight away from the Earth. Environmental spokespeople are promoting lab-grown food as a solution to the nightmare of industrial agriculture. So-called 'progressive' think-tanks envision a climate-deranged world in which humanity has "adapted" by moving into polar latitudes and building megacities with populations 2.5 times denser than Manila (today's densest metropolis), while importing energy and raw materials from the abandoned tropics and subtropics.[3]

I implore all my fellow young nature-lovers and activists to consciously reject—wholesale—the corporate-led, techno-globalist future we are being sold. Such suggestions represent yet another extension of the reductionist thinking and scientific hubris that originally justified exploitation of the biosphere—it's what got us into this mess in the first place. Tech-based "solutions" are still failing to curb emissions and unsustainable consumption, even as they guzzle more resources and damage more ecosystems in order to operate.[4] Moreover, they are fundamentally about enabling the continuation of a gargantuan global economy that can't even serve our own wellbeing, let alone that of the animals and ecosystems we love.

We've already seen how economic globalization undermines livelihoods and drives competition for ever-scarcer jobs, while exploiting workers and resources. We've felt the depression and stress it causes, as it rips apart community fabric and pressures us to compete at school and in the workplace. We're angry at the way it creates enormous wealth for the few at the expense of the many, and perpetuates the deep racial, cultural and economic injustices that are embedded in the colonial roots of the global economy. We've felt the emptiness of the consumer culture, suffered the serious health effects of the addictions in which it entraps us, and experienced the isolation and competitive rat-race of life in big cities.

We need to overcome the serious delusion that industrial modernity is the only way. The toxic cocktail of corporate globalization, high-tech development and urbanization is not inevitable, and it cannot offer any meaningful solution to the crises it has created.

What to do then?

Move onto the land, fight fire and pray that we too don't go up in flames?

Well, not quite. We have to go beyond the "fighting" response: the kind of response that saw Australian authorities bomb forests with thousands of tons of toxic fire-retardants and thousands of gallons of seawater last summer. This added insult to injury, poisoning the already-vulnerable waterways, ecologies and human communities. [5] No—we cannot simply invest in more machines, technologies and large-scale infrastructure to fight Nature.

A very different response is needed—one that is holistic, systemic, creative and actually works *alongside* natural processes, rather than against them. We are called to wake up to humanity's potential to *heal* the Earth: to restore her ecosystems, rebuild her soils, retain freshwater and draw down carbon.

This means getting over the myopic idea that humanity can only leave a destructive footprint on the Earth—an idea that depressed and paralyzed me when I was a teenager, and continues to torment too many nature-lovers. Let's open our eyes to the majority of human cultures—including and especially indigenous Australian ones—that have consistently *enriched* the biosphere. As ground-breaking books like *Dark Emu* and *Fire Country* reveal, indigenous people have been improving ecological health and abundance for millennia, by observing and listening to the ecosystems they inhabit, and altering them with small-scale agriculture and locally-sensitive resource-management.

Fundamental to the deep ecological wisdom of indigenous cultures are localized, land-based economies, in which human flourishing is directly tied to local ecological abundance. Similarly, by localizing our economies in the modern world, we can re-embed economy in ecology. We can set our resources (including our technological genius) to the task of maximizing ecological regeneration while simultaneously meeting all the needs of local communities. Homo sapiens can once again become Earth-healers.

Systemic Localization = Widespread Regeneration

For as long as I can remember, I have been searching for informed hope in light of the ecological crisis. My journey has been guided by author, environmentalist and alternative economist Helena Norberg-Hodge and her organization Local Futures, whose 2011 documentary *The Economics of Happiness* relieved me of the crippling idea that human flourishing and ecological wellbeing are separate, mutually-exclusive goals. It explained how localization is a "solution-multiplier" that rebuilds intimate, reciprocal relations between people, and between people and ecosystems.

Localizing our food systems, in particular, is the single most meaningful solution to climate breakdown. Sound like a big claim? Hear me out.

Most environmentalists are familiar with the fact that current agricultural practices are destructive on many levels. In the globalized food system, enormous quantities of uniform commodities are grown on vast, resource- and chemical-intensive monocultures and managed by fossil fuel-hungry agricultural machinery. Animals are raised in highly toxic and polluting factory farms. Harvests are flown around the world and back again just to be processed, packaged and sold. Soils are left bare and deadened, vulnerable to erosion by wind and rain. Farmers and farm workers are subjected to conditions constituting modern-day slavery.[6] All told, this food system is currently responsible for up to half of all anthropogenic greenhouse gas emissions,[7] as well as an immeasurable amount of deforestation, soil degradation, water consumption and biodiversity loss.

Localization flips this madness on its head. By localizing, we prioritize the production of a diversity of foods, fibers and medicines for local markets, stimulating a *seismic increase* in agricultural biodiversity. Farms come to act like natural ecosystems, returning organic matter to the soil and thereby boosting its carbon sequestration potential. Preliminary studies suggest that, if instituted on all the world's cultivated and pasture land, such agricultural systems could sequester over 100% of current global carbon emissions[8], while producing many more times (some studies show as much as 20 times) the amount of food per acre.[9]

And the benefits go far beyond just carbon drawdown. Agroecological farming techniques *bring the land back to life.* Allan Savory has convincingly shown how regenerative grazing of cows, goats and sheep has greened vast swathes of desertifying lands in Africa,[10] while Ernst Götsch was able to revive fourteen dry springs, reforest hundreds of hectares, and bring about more rainfall and cooler temperatures in his Brazilian microregion by mimicking the ecological succession of the surrounding forest, all while producing abundant food and lumber.[11]

How can farming possibly affect rainfall? The increased tree cover in diversified farms can seed the formation of clouds and reinforce wind patterns that bring the rain. And rebuilding soil turns it into a sponge for water, allowing rain to penetrate and refill aquifers, and soak into vegetation. Many small-scale farming systems also integrate water-retention landscapes, like community-managed percolation ponds, swales and wetland areas, which recharge groundwater and sustain rivers and springs. We should not underestimate the importance of these effects, especially since dried-up lands and depleted aquifers (thanks again in large part to industrial, globalized agriculture) was a central condition for both Australia and the USA's unprecedented fire seasons.[12]

There are still other forms of restoration and resilience that human beings can gift to their landscapes. As traditional fire practitioner Victor Steffensen details in *Fire Country*, indigenous custodians on this continent have worked with fire for many thousands of years, both to protect against wildfires and to actively enhance ecosystems. (Again, this parallels the situation in North America, where First Nations people also work with fire to both of these ends.[13]) They burn off dry shrubs, weeds, dead grasses and leaf litter in order to make way for new shoots to emerge and seeds to germinate. They burn slowly, coolly and in a piecemeal fashion (allowing animals to escape), making sure not to damage the canopy. They draw upon deep, intergenerational knowing of the land to choose the right times and places to burn, avoiding nesting seasons for ground-dwelling birds and fruiting seasons of key food sources. This is a hands-on approach, which aims not only to protect human beings, but to increase the biodiversity and life-giving capacity of entire ecosystems.

Let me stress why the broader framework of economic localization is so important for the needed revolution in agriculture and resource-management: all such methods need to be small in scale, slow in pace, and managed carefully by human hands. Diversified farms cannot be sowed or harvested by blind, standardizing machinery—they require the intimate care and sensitive cultivation that only human hands can offer. Similarly, practices like traditional fire management require more time—more hands and eyes per acre. Economic localization is a structural way to incentivize and revive this kind of small-scale, hands-on, job-rich, community-centered activity.

The cohesive fabric of local communities is, in and of itself, a form of social and ecological resilience—a force that can be mobilized to protect against natural disaster. In the Nimbin area of north-east New South Wales (a hotspot for intentional local communities), the Mt. Nardi bushfire threatened many homes and burnt through swathes of World Heritage protected Gondwanan rainforest. But the fire was contained thanks to a self-organized group of local eco-villagers, cooperative members and farmers called the Community Defenders.[14]

"Without the [Community Defenders'] work we would not have contained this fire" stated one fire brigade driver. "Man oh man, they stepped up in such a way that all of us in uniform were just completely blown away," praised the Captain, noting: "these communities are already intentional communities; there's already that fabric that exists there. I'm not too sure how that might work in a different area, where there are private leaseholds and people don't know their neighbors as well."

The Key Piece of the Puzzle

'Mitigation', 'adaptation', 'resilience' and 'regeneration'—these have become buzzwords in the environmental movement, and are increasingly present in policy discussions. But the key piece of the puzzle is left out far too often: any genuine climate solution requires *more hands on the land.*

This doesn't mean that you and I must quit our jobs, leave our social circles and move out to some rural backwater to start planting trees and growing our own food. While there are indeed countless brave young people doing that kind of pioneering work, we really need policy frameworks that facilitate localization so that it's not a constant uphill battle. This means policies that:

- make local food, clothing and building materials cheaper and more accessible than produce from the other side of the world,

- revitalize life in smaller cities and towns by providing good quality jobs, exciting education and cultural opportunities,

- shorten the distances between producer and consumer wherever possible, to allow more transparent, more accountable and more democratic economies,

- encourage small-scale, diversified production for local markets, rather than large-scale commodity production for export.

We could support the reconstruction of local, diversified economies in rural areas, while linking cities up with regional producers of basic needs. We could stop supporting globalized systems of production run by unaccountable corporations, and start investing in smaller businesses that are structurally able to adapt to local conditions, to participate in circular economies and to respect community relationships. This would mean redirecting economic subsidies, taxes and regulations away from supporting energy and technology, and towards favoring employment. For example:

- Instead of spending tens of millions of taxpayer dollars on leasing enormous water-bombing aircraft, we could employ people to carry out traditional burns, under the supervision of indigenous experts.

- With half the amount of money that currently subsidizes Big Ag, we could support farmers to transition to regenerative practices, and fund the establishment of many more small farms.

- Instead of pouring money into infrastructure for ever more global trade, we could strengthen local supply chains and rebuild the much lighter infrastructure needed for local markets and small businesses— think railways, post offices, public market spaces.

- Instead of signing "free trade" treaties that give multinationals still more freedom to do whatever they please, we could start reregulating them, while cutting the red tape and bureaucracy that too often strangles smaller players and community projects.

Just a couple of years ago, the very idea of policy change would have put off a lot of people (especially younger people). Back then, mainstream environmental and social justice messaging still focused on changing individual behaviors. But I am encouraged to see, on social media and in conversation with my peers, that there has been a marked shift. We are increasingly using our imaginations to reach beyond the depressing confines of neoliberal capitalism and industrial modernity, and we are realizing we have a collective democratic muscle to exercise. More than ever, we are up for the challenge of taking on systems change.

I therefore propose that our most urgent task is to envision land-based futures, and to demand that political steps be taken to realize them. Imagine: empowered and responsive communities and more small businesses meet water-retentive and flood-resilient landscapes, informed land-management, biodiverse farms and enlivening ecosystems. These elements can intersect to form the fabric of our future; a fabric that can hold us in safety and profound optimism, even as the specter of climate change looms.

This goes far beyond transitioning the current global economy to renewables; if we're honest with ourselves, we know our love for Nature goes much deeper than that. It envisions human societies reintegrated into the natural world, sustained by food forests and holistically managed ecosystems, powered by small-scale, community-owned renewables. It blurs the line between the wild and the cultivated, between the human and the non-human, between the individual and the universe.

A Latent Capacity for Healing

Over the months since the rains finally came and extinguished the fires, one of my greatest joys has been to witness the incredible regenerative capacity of burnt forests. With water at their roots, the blackened bodies of eucalypt and banksia, paperbark and bloodwood burst into bright pink and green leafy shoots. Grasstrees and ferns sprang from the ashy ground. Forests turned from somber graveyards to vibrant palaces of chlorophyll, and lyrebirds could still be found scratching through the slowly regenerating soil.

My solace is that we humans—even the scientists among us—cannot fully understand the incredible regenerative capacity of our planet. Therefore, we can hold out hope that the dire scientific models and predictions of the future are not the full picture. I believe, if we shift our global economic system towards a plurality of systems that support the hands-on cultivation and renewal of ecosystems, and if we shift our cultures towards Earth-reverence rather than Earth-oppression, we can have faith that Mother Earth may move in surprising ways to rebalance the global climate and support life. Dare I say, she actually *wants* to do so.

If that sounds naïve, remember that scientific hubris has always been ecological enemy number one—we thought Nature was mechanical and predictable, able to be dissected, predicted and manipulated. But now, even science is moving in a more holistic direction. We are learning that things as tiny as atoms are fundamentally unpredictable—in the words of Rupert Sheldrake, they have an *innate freedom*. Surely then, so do ecosystems, ocean currents and weather systems.

Indigenous people the world over tell of conscious powers embedded in mountains, rivers, forests and seas. What if moving beyond the dire scientific predictions of out-of-control ecological death-spirals and climate time bombs, and collectively dedicating ourselves to a more beautiful future, could incite these powers to reawaken? We have never understood the true complexity of the living world. By stepping into that humility, and by embodying faith in the untold power and intentionality of Mother Earth to support life, we may just release a cascade of regenerative power that we scarcely dare to imagine.

After the fires, I was humbled to see how some trees exploded into new shoots after a week or two, while others of the same species and in the same areas took months. The complexity and uniqueness of all the life around us denies reductionist categorization—we simply cannot fully understand the nature of Nature.

What we can do, however, is to raise the call for an economics of humility; an economics that respects the diversity and dynamic flows of the natural world; an economics of localization. We can work to deconstruct the "invisible hand" of the global techno-economic juggernaut, and make it release its death grip from Nature's throat. In the humbled understanding that the Earth has what it takes to flourish, we can put our own hands to work in bringing her back to life.

If we do these things, we can believe in a future of expanding rainforests, flowing rivers, diverse species and a stable climate. We can believe in a world without famine or drought, without systemic violence or economic injustice. In the words of Charles Eisenstein, we can believe in the more beautiful world our hearts know is possible.

September 24, 2020

THE GREAT DECELERATION
Alex Jensen

D ownscaling the economy is not only necessary to save and perhaps enable regeneration of our beleaguered earthly home; it is also a genuinely humane, anti-poverty agenda. This may sound counter-intuitive to those marinading in trickle-down theory.

Upsetting the great acceleration juggernaut will require innumerable, profound systemic shifts. Since the current system is the cause, not consequence, of consumerism, acquisitiveness, separation, alienation, etc., we will first and foremost need to resist the forces that relentlessly propagate it—stopping corporate plunder of all sorts (from mines to minds); stopping and revoking neoliberal "free trade" agreements; breaking up and dismantling corporate-state power and the legal frameworks that underpin it; and, challenging the fundamentalist logic of unlimited growth. Rejecting the great acceleration will simultaneously require the (re)construction of radical alternative systems rooted in environmental ethics, ecological integrity, social justice, decentralization and deep democracy, beauty, simplicity, cooperation, sharing, slowness, and a constellation of related eco-social-ethical values.

But where will the motive to resist and regenerate come from, if the values of commercialized growth societies—competition, individualism, narcissism, nihilism, avarice—are so deeply indoctrinated? How can the opposite values be resuscitated after decades or centuries of anesthetization and repression? The fact is that all over the world there has always been and continues to be tremendous push-back against the system and support for countless alternatives. This is testament not only to human resilience and common sense but to the utter asynchrony of our current system with the genuine well-being of people.

To acknowledge and celebrate this spirited and widespread push-back is not to be complacent or naïve about the terrifying hegemony and momentum of the great acceleration. It is, rather, precisely to disrupt the complacency and debilitation of inevitablism.

Thankfully, all over the world, vibrant movements of resistance-(re) construction both new and ancient are saying loudly, "we are ready to stop being trickled-down upon." The Degrowth movement is assailing the status quo assumption of a cozy, positive relationship between economic growth and well-being and even (weirdly) environmental "improvement". Its many exponents and activists are broadcasting the reality of the obvious-to-all-but-economists inverse relationship between growth and well-being. Given that the economy today is vastly exceeding what the planet and its denizens can give and take, degrowth—as its name suggests—promotes not merely slowing and stopping growth but reversing it.

At centers like Can Decreix on the Mediterranean coast of France,[1] the main argument of degrowth—that well-being improves and life becomes richer through sufficiency, commoning and technological-material downscaling—is practiced, demonstrated and shared. Human muscle and craft skills reclaim from machines simple, pleasurable subsistence work, done communally. Heat energy from the sun is used to bake bread and warm water. Music and fun are no longer things that must be purchased on weekends but instead are part of the fabric of everyday life. But it is not merely an escapist, "live your values while the world burns" sort of experiment; on the contrary, its members are deeply involved in the broader political struggles (e.g. against "free trade" treaties) that are a necessary corollary to living alternatively.

There are also many sister concepts and movements to degrowth that, despite their differences, share some basic, fundamental values and perspectives. There is Buen Vivir/Sumak Kawsay, emerging out of indigenous, eco-centric Andean cosmovisions, calling not for alternative development but alternatives *to* development. They encourage the affirmation and strengthening of traditional practices, knowledge systems, processes and relationships (human and non-human alike) that since time immemorial have embodied many of the qualities that movements in industrialized locales are striving to re-create.[2] On the Andean Altiplano, most Aymara and Quechua farming families still nurture, process and eat a spectacular varietal diversity of tubers, grains, legumes and other foods. One farmer I stayed with near Lake Titicaca grew 109 varieties of potato, plus dozens more of oca, olluco, mashua, quinoa, edible lupine, fava, wheat, barley, maize, and much more. He and his family, like the majority of other farming families there, provide most of their own milk, cheese, meat and wool from livestock like cows, alpacas, goats and sheep. They live in houses fashioned from adobe bricks of local clay, roofed with local grass thatch. Their young children know dozens of wild medicinal plants. They do all this not as heroic, isolated survivalists but in webs of community and earthly relationships of community, mutual aid, sharing and care. These communities have met their needs through local-regional economies—many based in barter—for centuries.[3] Are they thus perfect and free of all troubles? Of course not. But many of their worst troubles have been imposed by capitalist industrialism and other forces of "progress".

Perhaps the signal movement synthesizing resistance and (re) construction, ancient and contemporary, South and North, is the food sovereignty movement. This movement turns 500 years of colonialist food policy on its head. Colonialist systems encouraged people to give up their food autonomy and diverse traditions and either move into cities to become factory proletarians or, if remaining in the country-side, to become plantation proletarians. It forced local economies to export food, water, and labor power in exchange for paltry wages with which to shop for packaged "food-like stuff" in a global agribusiness supermarket. Yet, the food sovereignty movement inveighs against the political-economic forces that continue the war against peasants and subsistence economies. The movement demonstrates again and again the superiority (health, nutrition, productivity, ecological, social) of diverse, small, localized, cooperatively-worked, integrated polycultures of the sort that characterized food systems before factories were imposed onto the land.[4]

These and many other movements are pointing the way back from the abyss into which the great acceleration has hurled us, directing us towards the Great Deceleration necessary to live again with affection and beauty on this earth.

December 2, 2016

EDUCATING FOR A NEW ECONOMY
Helena Norberg-Hodge with Henry Coleman

"Tell me and I may forget; show me and I may not
remember; involve me and I will understand."
— First Nations Proverb

I n 1934, the Dean of Stanford University, Ellwood Cubberley, wrote:
"Our schools are, in a sense, factories, in which the raw materials [children] are to be shaped and fashioned into products. The
specifications for manufacturing come from the demands of 20th-century civilization, and it is the business of the school to build its pupils
according to the specifications laid down."[1]

Thankfully, there has been a marked shift in many countries around
the world away from the industrial, patriarchal values enshrined in
Cubberley's factory model of schooling. In various spheres of life—from
schooling to farming to home—there's been an embrace of more spiritual, humane and ecological values. We are seeing diversity, creativity
and indigeneity celebrated. We are witnessing a growing desire among
all kinds of people to weave deeper relationships with Nature and with
one another. Even in mainstream school systems, these changing values
are emerging, as inspired teachers pioneer curriculum reforms and
more holistic approaches.

However, there is still an entrenched link between education and
the economic system. And even though cultural values have shifted, the
economic system has continued in the direction of ever-larger-scale,
globalized extraction, and ever-deeper exploitation of people and the
natural world. In step with this acceleration, western-style schooling
has been exported to every corner of the globe. It encourages extreme
individualism and competition, and trains people in the technological
skills and worldview they need in order to be admitted to the global
economic order.

This schooling stands in stark contrast to Indigenous ways of
education, which tend to be intergenerational, collaborative, and
experiential. This became clear to me from living in the traditional

culture of Ladakh in the 1970s and 80s. In traditional Ladakh, children grew up surrounded by people of all ages, from young babies to great-grandparents—they were part of a whole chain of relationships. In this intergenerational context, I saw how they were naturally inclined to help one another—the eight-year-old teaching the five-year-old, who in turn lent a helping hand to the two-year-old.

Children learned from grandparents, family, and friends—often by *doing*—by imitating their elders. They learned and experienced connections, process, and change: the intricate web of fluctuating relationships in society and the natural world around them. From toddlers to grandparents, everyone took part in producing food, helping with irrigation, harvesting, and herding animals, as well as building houses, gathering fuel, and a host of other tasks essential to survival. Such skills required manual dexterity and great physical strength, along with a keen, creative mind and intellect. It also required location-specific, ecological knowledge, that allowed them, as they grew older, to use resources in an effective and sustainable way. In short, education nurtured an intimate relationship with the living world.

This all began to change when western-style education came to Ladakh in the 1970s. In the modern schools, none of the cultural or ecologically adapted knowledge was provided. Children were instead trained to become specialists in a technological monoculture. School was a place to forget traditional skills and, worse, to look down on them. Children were fined for speaking their own language instead of English or Hindi. They were told by their teachers that their traditional culture was backward. Meanwhile, they learned how to measure the angle that the Leaning Tower of Pisa makes with the ground and struggled with English translations of the *Iliad*.

To this day, school curricula are very similar—from Ladakh to London, from New York to Nairobi. Thanks again to the economic pressures that come from the global economic order, studies are increasingly focused on 'STEM' subjects, computer programming, public-relations, and business management: skills that grease the cogs of what can be described as a global techno-economic machine. But even more important than what is included is *what is left out*. The world over, modern education is educating people out of the skills they need to survive and thrive in their own cultures and regions, omitting any mention of generations of ecological knowledge and practical, land-based skills. At the same time, it fails to promote wellbeing and holistic thinking, and actively removes people from full participation in the real, living world.

In the modern education system, agricultural "experts" don't learn how to nourish people—they learn about chemical-intensive techniques to mass-produce commodities for export. Engineering and architecture graduates don't learn how to build houses from the materials that are abundantly available in local bioregions—they learn how to build using a narrow-range of energy-intensive manufactured commodities. The result is artificial scarcity. People worldwide end up competing for a narrow range of globally traded commodities—from fossil fuels and rare earth metals to wheat, corn, cement and plastic—while ignoring the relatively abundant resources of their own ecosystems.

Thus, in cities like Beirut and Dubai, air-conditioned skyscrapers with windows that don't open are replacing traditional forms of architecture that were designed for passive cooling. Across the world, housing developments are constructed of imported steel and plastic, while trees on site are razed and put through the woodchipper. Even as the use of terms like "regenerative", "biodiversity" and "ecological" abound, the biological deserts of industrial monocultures are replacing diversified, localized, sustainable food systems. Such examples epitomize the ecological blindness of over-specialized knowledge for universal application. They also illustrate the systemic escalation of resource-use, pollution and waste that emanates from a globalized, industrialized economy. Through the education-industrial complex, global replaces local, urban replaces rural, monoculture replaces diversity, consumerism replaces culture, fossil fuels and technology replace people, competition replaces community. This globalizing system is taking us away from Nature, away from each other, and away from ourselves.

As I mentioned at the outset, however, the schooling system has not been able to quash the intuitive intelligence of countless people around the world, who are doing their best to steer education and the economy in a very different direction. Despite widespread westernization, industrialization, and urbanization—or actually *in reaction to* them—there is a growing recognition of our innate spiritual connection to community and to Nature. Similarly, people are realizing that learning essential skills like growing food are beneficial for the development of both body and mind.

A vital movement can be seen growing at the grassroots on every continent, even as it pushes against the grain of the dominant economic system. It involves a huge range of initiatives—from permaculture-based education to Steiner and Montessori schools, from community-schooling to wilderness-immersion experiences. Meditation, collaboration, art, music and dance are respected and practiced. Forest schools, edible school yards, classroom kitchens, and other more practical forms of education, abound. All such projects—broadly termed "alternative"—offer more place-based, hands-on, experiential, ecological, collaborative educational experiences. They represent a small, relatively silent revolution, reversing centuries of de-skilling. Whether consciously or not, this alternative education movement is acting in tandem with transformative steps towards a new economy—towards more spiritual, Nature- and community-based, localized ways of life. It imagines a future in which human beings are much more than left-brains performing narrow, manipulative tasks in front of screens. By allowing human hands, hearts and minds to act as a cohesive, creative whole, this grassroots movement is preparing people to contribute to communities that have control over their own food systems, their own economies, and their own lives.

In the words of First Nations Nishnaabeg scholar Leanne Simpson, the revitalized Nishnaabewin knowledge system "does not prepare children for successful career paths in a hyper-capitalistic system. It is designed to create self-motivated, self-directed, community-minded, interdependent, brilliant, loving citizens, who at their core uphold our ideals around family, community and nationhood by valuing their intelligences, their diversity, their desires and gifts and their lived experiences." [2]

In light of learnings from Ladakh and from many other Indigenous cultures, an education system that ensures the future wellbeing of our planet and of its people will look more ancient than modern. That transition can start at multiple levels. For example:

- In early education, parents and community members can be actively included. Kindergartens can be brought together with old people's homes in symbiosis—perhaps in outdoor settings and in community gardens. In this way, the elderly can receive more of the connection they need to remain fit and healthy, while children are allowed to play more freely in Nature, under watchful, caring eyes.

- In higher education, more interdisciplinary modes of investigation can be funded, and the status of experiential knowledge can be elevated—as opposed to the current focus on information deduced through abstracted, reductionist datasets. Specialization and corporate funding can be challenged and rolled back.

- In saying that, genuine systemic transformation can only be achieved if many more of us participate in a rather different kind of education. We call it "education-as-activism". This is not about educating our children, but about educating ourselves to see the connections that are not obvious in our anonymous global structures. Education-as-activism involves:

- Unlearning some basic assumptions that have been drummed into us through schooling and mainstream media. For example, questioning the ideas of "progress" and "development", and revising our understanding of human nature, wellbeing and knowledge.

- Becoming more literate in economics, by developing a basic understanding of the skewed subsidies, taxes and regulations that have abetted global corporate expansion.

- Examining how the large-scale, globalized economic system inevitably increases resource use, widens the gap between rich and poor, and jeopardizes personal and societal wellbeing.

- Learning about the profound ways that place-based, localized economies can heal our societal and environmental wounds. Seeing why smaller scale economic and political systems—based on transparent, reciprocal relations—are needed to respect biological and cultural diversity.

- Reawakening our deeper spiritual selves. Pausing to listen to our hearts and our embodied wisdom. Allowing ourselves to feel the joy of connection to the deeper dance of life, to let go of the need to master, to control, to label and "know".

This is about resisting the dominant ideology and actively disseminating a different vision. We need our analytical, left-brain faculties to examine and articulate the flaws in global economic structures, and to go up against mainstream "experts" and prevailing dogmas with robust argumentation. In doing so we need to be guided by a deeper, more intuitive right-brain knowing, an embodied wisdom that leads us towards genuinely empathetic and joyous relations with ourselves, with others and with all of creation.

October 19, 2021

FROM GLOBAL TO LOCAL IN INDIA
Alex Jensen

A ubiquitous billboard for a tech company neatly captures the zeitgeist in modern-day Bangalore, and in rapidly-urbanizing India generally: *The Future is Fast. We are Faster.*
Today, Bangalore's erstwhile appellation as India's "garden city" seems sadly anachronistic. Along with bumper-to-bumper traffic, there are glamorous shopping malls and an exploding, bewildering skein of real estate developments, garbage mountains, and slums. The air quality is truly mephitic from the collective emissions of millions of vehicles, factories, and garbage fires. Such are some of the characteristics of the modern Indian megacity, a rude foil to the Panglossian image of progress presented by the official boosters of globalization, urbanization and growth.

Despite the pace of "development" in India, it is also true that much more of the vernacular, the traditional, and the independent hangs on here than in many countries. Even in the middle of major cities, large quantities of food and other daily needs are still supplied from tiny independent local shops or street vendors, and local craftsmen (weavers, potters, tinkers, tailors, etc.) ply their trades in the enormous "informal" sector. Multinational chain restaurants like KFC and McDonald's—while now ubiquitous in the affluent parts of cities—have not displaced stubbornly popular local eateries, and local alternatives to corporate junk food persist everywhere. And in spite of economic, trade and development policies that relentlessly conspire against them, small farmers still make up the majority of the population, and most of the food is still provided by them.[1]

Because it still retains so much of the traditional and land-based, India is arguably better-positioned than the West to forge an alternative path to the future—one based on principles of economic localization. Despite the grievous losses to seed and food diversity occasioned by decades of imposition of industrial agriculture, an enormous amount remains intact, as illustrated at a recent seed festival and an amazing Adivasi (indigenous) food festival. There is a vibrant sustainable food and farming movement to protect and promote this diversity,[2] and GMO trials can still be stopped here[3] (Monsanto's Bt cotton is the only commercially grown GMO, though the petroleum/ environment minister is working overtime to change that).

Though the political establishment is dutifully working to roll out the red carpet for the big boxes, corporate retail has yet to fully penetrate, and faces formidable resistance from small shopkeepers.[4] Farmers and tribal groups are courageously agitating against industrial land take-overs in dozens of states.

Most critically, countless groups and individuals are arising to confront the development monster—to actively challenge its assumptions and impositions, and to regenerate dying traditions and nontoxic local economies that rely on local resources. And there is vibrant resistance and renewal work happening all over the subcontinent that comprises, in essence, a massive localization movement.

The Economics of Happiness Conference in Bangalore provided a platform from which to launch an exciting new part of that movement, an India-wide initiative called Alternatives India (*Vikalp Sangam* in Hindi).[5] The initiative asks this basic question: "As the world hurtles towards greater ecological devastation, inequalities, and social conflicts … are there alternative ways of meeting human needs and aspirations, without trashing the earth and without leaving half of humanity behind?" Their answer is a resounding yes, and they point to "a multitude of grassroots and policy initiatives: from meeting basic needs in ecologically sensitive ways to decentralized governance and producer-consumer movements, from rethinking urban and rural spaces towards sustainability to struggles for social and economic equity." Alternatives India is a platform to highlight, connect, and thereby strengthen the country's diverse profusion of local initiatives that are charting a saner course into the future for India.

Perhaps the future of India is not fast and faster after all, but slow and local.

May 28, 2014

TOSEPAN:
RESISTANCE AND RENEWAL IN MEXICO
Alex Jensen

S ince the mid-1980s, Mexico has been a poster child for globalization. Through free trade treaties and structural adjustment policies
imposed by international financial institutions, the country has
been "liberalized"—opened up to unfettered corporate investment and
imports—to an extent matched by few other countries. Though the
North American Free Trade Agreement (NAFTA) is the most well-
known trade treaty to affect Mexico, it is but the first and largest of
numerous multilateral and bilateral agreements that make Mexico the
world's free trade agreement (FTA) leader. All told, Mexico has signed
12 free trade agreements with 44 nations, 28 bilateral investment treaties, and 9 agreements of economic cooperation.[1]

The grim consequences of globalization in Mexico are by now familiar. NAFTA threw the doors open to heavily subsidized US agribusiness
products—especially corn—which subsequently flooded into the country. Imports increased three-fold, and the price of corn dropped 50
percent, devastating the rural economy and forcing some 4.9 million
campesinos (peasants) out of farming altogether, precipitating their mass
migration from the countryside to cities (and to the US) in order to
survive.[2]

NAFTA also exposed the Mexican economy to retail and fast-food
multinationals based in the US, besieging the country with an avalanche
of junk foods and soft drinks high in fat, salt, and sugar, and an atten-
dant epidemic of deadly "diet-related diseases"—e.g. hypertension,
diabetes, and obesity (these would be more accurately termed "corporate globalization-related diseases").[3]

The liberalization regime has also fueled a veritable bonanza for
extractive industries—from mining and fossil fuels to big dams and
mega-infrastructure developments. Transnational companies—with
the blessing of state and national governments—have been scouring the
country, extracting its natural wealth and concentrating the benefits in

fewer and fewer corporate hands (the richest 1 percent in Mexico owns over half of the country's wealth).[4] Consequently, Mexico hosts over 500 ongoing environmental conflicts—one of the highest counts in the world today.[5] Defenders of the environment are targeted with violent reprisals by those pushing destructive development. Global Witness reports that 15 environmental defenders were killed in Mexico in 2017, up from 3 in 2016.[6]

Unión de Cooperativas Tosepan

It is hard to find much hope amidst this desperate situation, and yet, throughout Mexico, there is a florescence of inspiring resistance and alternatives, some long-established, some only now springing up. In the southern state of Puebla, the lush, cloud-forested Sierra Norte mountains bordering Veracruz are home to one of the oldest and most inspiring of these movements of "the other Mexico" or *México profundo*: the Unión de Cooperativas Tosepan (Also known as *Tosepan Titataniske*, meaning "United We Will Overcome", in Náhuatl).[7]

In Puebla, local communities defending their territories and lifeways are confronting corporate-state development projects, including mining, gas fracking, centralized electrical grid infrastructure, big dams, and big box stores. According to the EJ Atlas, concessions have been granted in Puebla for 11 mines and 14 hydroelectric projects, along with petroleum development (including fracking).[8]

But there has been a fierce backlash across the state, successfully blocking many of these projects. In the Sierra Norte, the resistance has been particularly spirited and effective, causing a number of hydropower projects to be suspended, and a planned Walmart (under its Mexican subsidiary name, Bodega Aurrerá) to be scuppered.

Some of the most effective resistance has emanated from a network of cooperatives called Tosepan that has been working in the region for 40 years, building up a parallel solidarity economy among largely Nahua and Tutunaku indigenous communities, encompassing some 35,000 members across 430 villages in 29 municipalities. Tosepan was instrumental in encouraging a citizen's plebiscite to reject the incursion of a Walmart/Bodega Aurrerá store in the town of Cuetzalan in 2010, by using arguments about the economic, cultural and environmental harms it would cause.[9] An analysis was done showing that Walmart's promised 60 low-quality jobs would come at the cost of 500 local businesses, and put at risk the entire solidarity economy built up by Tosepan and others, based on ancestral indigenous practices.[10]

The significance of this victory cannot be overstated in a country where Walmart has steadily been taking over and dominating the economy (1 in 5 Walmart stores worldwide are in Mexico, destroying local livelihoods and spreading a culture of consumption, disposability, and waste).[11]

All of these struggles of resistance help to uphold the main work of Tosepan: constructing a holistic, sustainable, locally and democratically controlled economy rooted in the indigenous culture and knowledge of the Sierra Norte—a source of dignified livelihoods and ecological security, and a viable alternative to the distress-migration suffered by so many other communities.

Tosepan is comprised of three civil associations and eight cooperatives, which together cover basic needs. These include: organic agroecological farming of staples like corn, beans and vegetables, as well as crops like coffee, pepper, and sugarcane, both for sale (primarily to local markets) and for the community's subsistence; small-scale, community-based eco-tourism; natural building using local resources like bamboo and adobe, incorporating features like water harvesting, solar dehydrators, ecological cookstoves, and renewable energy; local healthcare, focusing on prevention and traditional herbal remedies; decentralized renewable energy with a goal of total energy sovereignty; and local finance to support the functioning of the entire ecosystem of cooperatives (Tosepan has its own cooperative bank, called *Tosepantomin*, meaning "money of all"/"everyone's money", in Nahuatl).[12]

Since 2001, Tosepan's members have been involved in organic coffee production based on highly diversified, biologically rich agroecological "gardens of coffee" that are possibly the most diversified coffee farms in Mexico. A single hectare may contain over 200 species of plants, with multiple ecological and social functions and values (ritual, medicinal, fuel, food for family consumption, non-timber forest products for trade, etc.).

Beginning in 2014 there has been a special emphasis on food sovereignty in Tosepan, with the goal of meeting local needs first. Some of the activities towards this end have included:

- increasing production of organic corn

- establishing vegetable gardens and chicken coops in the majority of member homes

- designing a local credit scheme called "Backyard Garden Credit"

- producing a documentary film, *Corazones de Maíz* (Hearts of Corn)

- writing a recipe book for wild greens/amaranth greens

- holding tastings to rescue and share traditional foods

- organizing events to barter backyard garden produce as well as seeds of corn, beans, amaranth, chilis and squashes

- maintaining a nursery with approximately 1 million plants—valuable forest species like coffee, macadamia, red cedar, cinnamon and many others—distributed each year to members for reforestation and agroforestry

- growing edible mushrooms on coffee pulp

Beginning in 2003, one of Tosepan's signature efforts has been to bring back the native bee *Scaptotrigona Mexicana*, known in the region as *pisilnekmej*. This bee was domesticated in pre-colonial times, and the unique system of two-tiered clay pot hives has been maintained since then. The bees' honey, propolis, and wax have many medicinal properties, while the pollen is rich in proteins. The cooperative also makes products like shampoos, soaps and creams from the honey and wax.

One of Tosepan's members, María Luisa Albores, explains the ethos guiding Tosepan's work: "Our cooperative model is based in values of a cosmovision or form of life that closely coincides with the social and solidarity economy which values life, people, the land, plants, and animals. From this vision we have constructed the mode of life of Tosepan.... The sense of belonging and permanence in our territory gives us identity...in the face of the onslaught and displacements of the capitalist system. Here we are and will continue with dignity, on foot walking in our land, which is sacred." [13]

The capitalist system's relentless need to expand and grow continues to pose a threat, and Tosepan has not been spared the violence that the global economy inflicts on local people standing in its way. Some of its leaders have been murdered and others have narrowly escaped attempts on their lives by mercenaries in the pay of industry.[14] Violence and physical intimidation, it seems, continue to be favored tools of plunderers who have otherwise been blocked by well-organized communities deeply committed to defense of their homes.

This is one of the signal lessons of the inspiring work of Tosepan: that a culture of solidarity—fortified by cooperatives providing for material and cultural needs—deepens democracy, and that this in turn makes it very hard for predatory capital to enter. However inspiring and admirable, though, the corporate free-trade regime bearing down on Mexico continues to hover menacingly in the background, posing a constant threat to any initiatives in local self-reliance, ecological security, dignity, and renewal. Thus the need to confront and dismantle this regime is still paramount, to enable many more Tosepans to emerge and succeed.

January 26, 2019

6

Local Food:
A Solution-Multiplier

THE CASE FOR LOCAL FOOD
Helena Norberg-Hodge

I f you want to create a more sustainable society, a good place to start is by helping to rebuild your local food economy. Food is something everyone, everywhere, needs every day, which means that even relatively small changes in the way it is produced and marketed can have immense effects. And since eating is a natural part of daily life, we all have frequent opportunities to make a difference.

Strengthening local food economies around the world protects small farms, businesses, and local jobs. It allows food to be produced in ways that nurture rather than destroy the land. And, if widespread enough, it would provide everyone with enough to eat—food that is as healthy and nutritious as possible.

Rebuilding local food economies means, most of all, shortening the distance food travels from farm to table. This doesn't mean putting an end to all trade in food or doing without oranges and bananas in cold climates. It simply means limiting the needless transport of food by trying to meet as many of our basic needs as possible, closer to home.

Many urbanized people have lost touch with the sources of their food and may not realize that the distance their food travels has been steadily increasing. In the US, the average pound of food now travels 1,500 miles before it reaches the dinner table, and the distance continues to grow.[1]

Much of this transport is needless: every day, identical commodities pass in opposite directions, criss-crossing the globe. The "logic" of the global economy leads the US and other nations to import hundreds of thousands of tons of staple foods each year, while simultaneously exporting roughly the same amount.[2] In an era of dwindling fossil fuel reserves and rising $CO2$ emissions, this is both senseless and wasteful. But it is a trend that is accelerating as governments systematically promote a single, globalized food system.

Within that food system, farming is merely an industry, and food is just another commodity. A misplaced emphasis on "efficiency" leads crops to be grown on huge farms specializing in one crop, and animals to be raised by the millions in closely confined conditions on factory farms. Along with the needless transport of food, the use of heavy equipment, toxic agrochemicals, and genetically modified seeds takes a heavy toll on the environment and belies any claim to efficiency.

These trends do not benefit farmers. "Free trade" policies are forcing local farmers to compete with farmers on the other side of the world, many of whom work for a pittance. At the same time, they are being squeezed between the huge agribusinesses that supply their inputs and those that buy their production. As a result, small farmers are going bankrupt all over the world, and rural communities are being drained of life. For US farmers, suicide is now the leading cause of death.

The quality of our food, meanwhile, is declining. Hormones and antibiotics are given to animals to make them grow rapidly and to keep them alive under inhumane factory conditions. Heavily processed global foods have been so stripped of flavor and aroma that chemical compounds designed to fool our senses must be added. Still others are added as preservatives to artificially extend shelf life, and foods may be irradiated with the same goal in mind. Already, roughly two-thirds of the products on US supermarket shelves contain genetically-modified ingredients.[3]

Further globalizing and industrializing our food supply is foolhardy and reckless. More sensible by far would be to shift direction and, instead, support more localized food production and marketing. Such a shift would bring immense benefits:

- Local food means fresher food, which in turn means healthier food. Fresh organic vegetables are on average ten times more nutritious than conventional supermarket vegetables.

- Marketing locally reduces the number of middlemen and therefore increases farmers' incomes. It also helps to cut prices, giving even low-income groups access to fresh affordable food.

- Local food systems lead to stronger local economies by providing jobs, supporting local shops, and keeping money from being siphoned off by distant investors and corporations.

- Local food systems encourage farmers to diversify their production, thereby making it easier to farm organically. Intercropping and rotations can replace dangerous pesticides while on-farm waste like manure and crop residues can replace chemical fertilizers.

- By reducing the need for expensive inputs, farm diversification keeps more money in farmers' pockets. And unlike monocultural farmers, those who diversify are less susceptible to heavy losses from pest infestations or abnormal weather conditions like droughts or unexpected frosts.

- Reliance on smaller farms increases overall productivity since smaller farms are more productive per acre than larger farms. A shift towards smaller farms would thus provide more food and better food security worldwide.

- Smaller-scale, diversified farms serving local markets also provide better conditions for farm animals than large factory farms. There is less crowding, less dependence on long-distance transport, and less need for antibiotics and other drugs.

How can a shift towards the local happen? It is important to realize that government policies now systematically promote the global food system, and those policies need to change. "Free trade" treaties, subsidies for long distance transport, relaxed anti-trust laws, hidden export subsidies, and much more work to support global producers and marketers at the expense of smaller competitors.

Shifts in policy alone, however, will not be enough. In addition, a multitude of small and local steps will be needed to re-create and nurture healthier food systems. And for many years now, people have been taking those steps, experimenting and succeeding with direct marketing systems, including farmers markets, consumer co-operatives, community farms, and the Community Supported Agriculture (CSA) movement.

With CSAs, consumers in towns and cities link up directly with nearby farmers. In some cases, consumers purchase an entire season's produce in advance, sharing the risk with the farmer. In others, shares of the harvest are purchased in monthly or quarterly installments. Consumers usually have a chance to visit the farm where their food is grown, and in some cases their help on the farm is welcomed. While small farmers linked to the industrial system continue to fail every year at an alarming rate, CSAs are allowing small-scale diversified farms to thrive in growing numbers. The model has spread rapidly throughout Europe, North America, Australia, and Japan. In the United States, the number of CSAs has climbed from only two in 1986 to 200 in 1992, and more than 12,500 in 2007.[4]

Nonetheless, we in the Global North are a long way from re-establishing more localized food systems. It is helpful to keep in mind a tremendously hopeful point: even today, many of the world's people, mostly in the Global South, still live on the land, growing food for themselves, their families, and their own communities.

We need to do what we can to ensure that the economic and social structures on which those rural people depend are not further undermined. Insisting that people in the poor parts of the world devote their labor and their best land to feeding people on the other side of the planet does not ultimately benefit them. Feeding ourselves as much as possible while assisting the people of the Global South to diversify their economies—enabling them to feed themselves before they think about feeding us—would be the equitable thing to do.

As things stand today, part of every dollar we spend on transported food—and a sizable portion of our tax dollars—pays for food transport, packaging, advertising, processing, artificial flavors, chemical preservatives and toxic agrochemicals, as well as research into still more industrial food technologies. In return we're getting poor quality food, a degraded environment, and rural communities sapped of life. Is this how we want our money spent? If not, we should be resisting the further globalization of food by pressing for policy changes and by buying local, organic foods whenever possible.

There are few things more inspiring than contributing to the renewal of ecosystems and supporting the new generation of young farmers. If you get involved, you'll help to heal the planet, your community, and yourself.

August 27, 2010

7 BILLION FOR DINNER?
HERE'S HOW TO FEED THEM
Steven Gorelick

T he number of hungry people on the planet is on the rise. According to the FAO, 821 million people faced chronic food deprivation in 2017—the third consecutive year of increase.[1] The question arises: how can we feed 7 billion people on the planet's finite resources?

Most people, even many of those who support small farms and eat organic food, believe that there's no way to feed the global population without the use of chemical fertilizers and pesticides, fossil fuels, biotechnology, heavy equipment, and the rest of the agribusiness arsenal. In fact, the 2013 World Food Prize—which supposedly recognizes individuals who have improved "the quality, quantity or availability of food in the world"—went to three stalwarts of the biotech industry, including the Technology Officer of Monsanto and a lead scientist at Syngenta.[2] (This should have surprised no one, since the sponsors of the Prize include many of the world's largest food corporations, from Cargill, Archer Daniels Midland, PepsiCo, and Dupont Pioneer to the aforementioned Monsanto and Syngenta.)[3]

But the question really comes down to this: on the planet's limited stock of arable land, how can the most food be produced? There's no doubt where Local Futures stands: in our film *The Economics of Happiness* we point out that "small locally-adapted farms ... produce substantially more food per acre" than industrial farms. Vandana Shiva gave substance to that claim, pointing out that "research has shown, again and again and again, that bio-diverse small farms using ecological inputs produce three to five times more food than industrial monocultures."

This is not a new revelation. Our book *Bringing the Food Economy Home* cited a 1999 study showing that small farmers worldwide produce from 2 to 10 times more per unit area than do larger, corporate farms.[4] Nonetheless, there is a persistent myth that industrial agriculture is vastly more efficient than smaller, more diversified alternatives.

This belief rests entirely on a perverse definition of "efficiency". The efficiency touted by the promoters of industrial agriculture has nothing to do with producing large amounts of food on a limited landbase: it's about producing the highest yield *with the least amount of human labor.* In other words, industrial agriculture is *not* more efficient at producing food. It's more efficient at eliminating farmers and farmworkers. If the goal isn't to pull people off the land but to produce the most food, then small-scale, locally-adapted, diversified farms are the way to go.

Here's a real-life example of small-farm productivity from our place here in northern Vermont. It's less of a farm than a homestead, since most of the food we produce is consumed by our family of four or exchanged in an informal barter network with neighbors—though we do have a small "cash crop" of blueberries that we sell at a nearby farmers market and to a couple of local stores. Our garden area, including the blueberry patch, is less than a quarter-acre, large by backyard garden standards but miniscule in comparison to industrial monocultures.

The climate here isn't particularly favorable (this year we had four inches of snow at the end of May, and a frost by early September), but we always grow a huge supply of tomatoes, peppers, cucumbers, lettuce, spinach, beans, peas, scallions, summer squash, broccoli, cabbage, cauliflower, chard, kale, asparagus, and more. Along with the potatoes, carrots, beets, onions, garlic, winter squash, and celeriac in storage, we freeze, dry, can, or ferment enough other vegetables to meet most of our needs until the following year; frozen or preserved blueberries, raspberries, blackberries, apples and pears, meanwhile, provide us with copious amounts of fruit. Much of what we don't raise ourselves can be supplied by exchanging surpluses with neighbors.

I'm not saying this to boast since we're not particularly exceptional: lots of people in this part of Vermont have gardens even more productive than our own, and putting up food is a tradition that goes back many generations. What's more, our productivity would be dwarfed by that of small farmers in parts of the world—like Ladakh—where location-specific knowledge, building on centuries of direct experience of local conditions, is still intact. My point is only that a lot of food can be grown in a small area using nothing but on-farm inputs and human labor. It's very labor-intensive (just ask anyone in my family), but the food is not only plentiful, it's nutrient-dense, healthy, and delicious.

Yet this doesn't explain *why* smaller farms are more productive per acre than industrial monocultures. One reason is that diversified farms can use the same space to grow multiple crops. In our garden, for example, spinach, lettuce, and scallions grow from the same soil as the peas climbing the fencing above; beans grow between the rows of potatoes, and the vines from squash and cucumber plants quickly cover not only the garden paths but climb up the corn stalks and weave between the onions. And since we use only hand tools in the garden, we don't need to leave space for the tires of tractors and other mechanized farm equipment.

On our farm, even the garden weeds can be considered a crop. Some of them—dandelion, lamb's quarter, purslane, and others—are themselves edible and add to our diet. More importantly, the weeds we pull from the garden can be fed to our goats and cows, who turn them into milk and meat. In an industrial monoculture there are no animals to feed this volunteer crop to: instead, it is eliminated by chemical herbicides. Other garden "wastes"—corn husks, onion tops, empty bean pods, overripe blueberries, and so on—similarly become valuable feed for our animals, adding to the net productivity of the farm. There's even a use for the "harmful" insects in our garden ecosystem. Rather than spray pesticides to get rid of cut worms, Japanese beetles, grubs, or potato beetle larvae, we remove them by hand and feed them to our laying hens, which convert this protein-rich food into eggs.

Another reason small farms are more productive is that the machinery on which industrial farms depend can never be as knowledgeable or as careful as humans. When our family picks blueberries, for example, we know what each of the several varieties we grow look and feel like when they're perfectly ripe: berries that aren't quite ready will be left for the next day's picking, when they'll be larger, juicier, and better-tasting. But the mechanical blueberry-picking machines favored by large growers can't make such distinctions: they simply shake the entire bush and catch whatever berries drop. A University of Florida study showed that because mechanical harvesting bruises many good berries and harvests many under-ripe ones, it yields 13 percent less marketable fruit, with "significant [additional] losses from blue and immature fruit dropped on the ground by the harvester."[5] In other words, farms that use machines to pick their fruit get smaller harvests; nonetheless, they are described as more "efficient" because they use less human labor.[6]

When we planted our blueberries 15 years ago, we chose varieties that were well-suited to our farm's particular soils and micro-climate. If we had intended to use a mechanical harvester, however, we would have chosen different varieties—those that are better at withstanding machine harvesting—in order to minimize harvesting losses. All industrial-scale farmers are forced to make similar choices. What's more, they're also forced to choose from among the handful of crops and varieties favored by global markets. The result is that large farms tend to be adapted to technology and the market while small farms are adapted to nature. The former may produce the most money, but the latter produce the most food.

By choice, necessity, or both, small farmers around the world make the best possible use of the land available to them. When they don't rely on off-farm inputs, their "footprint" is often just the land itself. The footprint of industrial monocultures, by contrast, includes not only the land under cultivation, but the land from which their mineral inputs are mined, the factories where the herbicides and pesticides are manufactured, the labs where their biotech seeds are developed, and the vast global infrastructure of fossil fuels and highways needed to run their massive equipment and to transport the end product to global markets. On a finite planet, reducing all of these resource demands is critical.

Needless to say, labor-intensive small farms require a lot more farmers and farmworkers—a good thing in a world in which unemployment is a major problem. They also use far less fossil-fuel energy—also a good thing. Nonetheless, government policies continue to promote the further industrialization of agriculture—in part by subsidizing the cost of energy, which makes it cheaper to use machines than people. In the Global South, government "development" policies essentially pull millions of people—including some of the most productive farmers—off the land and dump them in urban slums. The result is both increased unemployment and farms that are less efficient. In Wendell Berry's apt phrase, those government policies "take a solution and divide it neatly into two problems".[7]

So, how can we best feed 7 billion people? With food from small, locally-adapted farms using ecological inputs, that's how.

November 24, 2013

IS LOCAL ORGANIC FOOD ELITIST?
Steven Gorelick

L ocal food solves a plethora of issues: it helps family farmers and other small businesses survive, thereby revitalizing rural economies; it minimizes the need for a wide range of inputs, from pesticides and chemical fertilizers to preservatives and packaging; it increases agricultural biodiversity, adding to long-term food security; and by reducing unnecessary food transport, it lessens our fossil fuel use and the pollution and greenhouse gas emissions that go with it. What's more, a shift from global to local food would benefit self-reliant villagers throughout the Global South while making healthy, nutritious food more abundant and more affordable everywhere.

With all this going for the local food movement, it can be disconcerting to hear some people argue that "local organic food is elitist." Disconcerting, but not surprising: for decades now, a handful of well-funded corporate front groups has been diligently working to link local organic food with "elitism", particularly in America, and their work is paying off.

One of these groups is the Center for Consumer Freedom (CCF), funded by Coca-Cola, Monsanto, Cargill, Tyson Foods, and others.[1] CCF's avowed mission is to shoot the messengers delivering unfavorable news about corporate products. According to a CCF spokesman, the group targets "just about every consumer and environmental group, chef, legislator or doctor who raises objections to things like pesticide use, genetic engineering of crops or antibiotic use in beef and poultry".[2] A favored means of eliminating these critics is to accuse them of elitism. CCF's website, for instance, features articles with headlines like "Opposition to Biotechnology: Elitism in its Cruelest Form"; another claims that those working to address America's obesity epidemic have "the elitist conviction that Americans can't be trusted to take care of themselves".[3]

CCF is not the only group spreading the elitism message. Dennis Avery of the right-wing Hudson Institute (with support from McDonald's, Monsanto, Dupont, and Exxon) calls environmentalists "affluent elites" who believe that "the world's poor should stay poor." [4] And Elizabeth Whelan of the agribusiness-funded American Council on Science and Health calls the organic food movement "elitist and arrogant". "The only thing healthy about organic food," she sniffs, "is the price." [5]

Although these groups promote the interests of big business, they attempt to give a humanitarian spin to their arguments. Prominent among their claims is the canard that industrial food is needed to feed the world's starving masses, even though it has been documented time and again that small-scale organic farms are far more productive per acre than their industrial counterparts. In any case, it is usually not a shortage of food that leads to hunger in the Global South, but development and trade policies—largely designed to benefit those same big businesses—that pull people away from self-reliant village economies and consign them to poverty in urban slums.

The elitism argument isn't limited to North-South relations. Another claim is that even in the Global North, only affluent elites can afford local organic food. Yes, industrial food usually sells for less than fresher, healthier food. But distantly-transported industrial food is actually quite costly if one accounts for all the direct and hidden subsidies our governments lavish on it, and it becomes still more expensive if one accounts for its many social and environmental costs. Local organic food—which is unsubsidized, has significant social benefits and far lower environmental costs—is the real bargain.

In the end, the agribusiness-led assault on local organic food does not rely on a strong argument, but on a subtle psychological ploy. The subtext of the elitism claim is that industrial food is central to the identities of average Americans. Criticizing the corporate-run system that produces this food thus becomes the equivalent of attacking the "ordinary people" who eat it.

This is a clever stratagem: simply eating Big Macs or microwave pizza makes you part of the solid, patriotic backbone of America, a defender of Mom and frozen apple pie. Choosing alternatives to industrial food, on the other hand, is equated with believing yourself better than everyone else: only an elitist with no respect for decent Americans or their mealtime rituals would challenge this or any other feature of the consumer culture, America's sacred way of life.

But there is nothing sacred about this culture. Unlike genuine traditions and cultural adaptations to place, the consumer culture is largely artificial, the creation of huge corporations that require masses of homogenized consumers for their products. It is the product of mammoth entertainment and media empires, billions of dollars in saturation advertising, and cradle-to-grave immersion in the belief that ever more consumption is the surest path to happiness. Corporate-funded think tanks help maintain this manufactured culture, spreading its ideology through propaganda that passes from pundits to the public like a virus.

Most serious critics of the consumer culture do not attack those whose lives are embedded in it. Instead, they challenge the economic and political structures that prop it up. Those structures help make industrial food ubiquitous and artificially cheap while limiting the availability of local organic food and making it comparatively expensive.

Here are some suggestions for challenging the consumer culture's food system while making local organic food more accessible to everyone, including the poor:

- First, eliminate the subsidies and tax breaks currently going to industrial food and shift them to small-scale production for local markets. The reason giant Slurpees are cheaper than local fruit juices, for example, is that industrial corn sweetener is highly subsidized while local apple juice gets no support all.

- Shift the massive government research and development funding that goes towards industrial production (biotechnology, pesticides, mechanization, etc.) towards research that would help small-scale organic farmers.

- Scale back the huge subsidies currently devoted to long-distance transport—in both the Global North and South—which make it easy and artificially cheap for distantly-produced foods to invade the markets of local producers. Devote that funding instead to the infrastructure needs of local food economies, like covered markets, community-based processing facilities, and small-scale renewable energy projects.

- Shift taxation away from labor and onto fossil fuels, thus reducing unemployment and pollution simultaneously. This would significantly raise the price of energy-intensive global food and reduce the price of labor-intensive local food.

- Re-regulate global corporations. As things stand now, "free trade" treaties and financial de-regulation enable global corporations to invade markets around the world. If communities were allowed to protect themselves from a flood of outside goods, local food economies would have a chance to flourish.

- Change the health and safety regulations that are currently strangling small, local producers and businesses. Though most of these have been enacted because of the abuses of large-scale businesses, they can make it almost impossible for smaller businesses to survive.

Far from elitist, these are steps towards an economy in which *everyone* has access to the freshest, healthiest food possible.

June 15, 2007

PEACHES HELP GROW
SLOVENIA'S GIFT ECONOMY
Marjana Kos

One summer day in Slovenia, a man decided to buy a box of peaches from a local farmer while on a business trip to Vipava—a fruit-growing region. He was very pleased about the price—1 euro per kg—which is roughly half the price in the shops. The farmer was even happier about the price, because this was almost 6 times the "global market price" he was getting from Fructal, the fruit juice factory in the region.

Because there was plenty of room in his van, the businessman offered to bring back boxes of peaches to others who might be interested. He posted his offer on Slovenia's "good deeds" portal (www.dobradela.si), and the offer spread quickly through email and Facebook. In the end he received several hundred requests for peaches—too many for him to handle. So he asked people for organizational help: receiving and sorting requests, picking up boxes from a central location in Ljubljana, and delivering them locally. An online sign-up system was set up virtually overnight, and dozens of people volunteered to help. Suddenly, a one-time offer became a nation-wide project.

As one might expect, he bumped into administrative barriers: he was told that "good deeds" are not recognized by law, and that he would have to pay tax on the money he collected from people—even though he would be receiving only what he paid for the peaches, without any profit. These barriers didn't stop him. Instead, he distributed the peaches for free! People were told that in exchange they could do something good for someone else.

More than five thousand people participated in the initiative, distributing over 10 tons of peaches throughout Slovenia. It was one of the biggest self-organized projects in the country, second only to the "Let's Clean Slovenia in One Day" campaign in 2010. And these peaches actually had taste: unlike those at supermarkets, they ripened on trees and were delivered to people virtually overnight.

The peach season is over, but the initiative continues: the core group is setting up a system that will be financially viable. Growers are already contacting them with offers for autumn fruits like grapes and apples, and people are using the system to distribute things for those in need, from toys and bicycles to clothes, computers, phones, and more.

Beyond village economies, localization is about forging more direct, more human-scale relationships and circumventing the global juggernaut. Most important, this spontaneous, self-organizing initiative is proof that people are motivated by far more than self-interest and profit.

September 28, 2013

YOUNG FARMERS IN LADAKH
Chozin Palmo, Jigmet Singge and Kunzang Deachen

L adakh—high on the Tibetan Plateau at the northern extreme of India—is the place we call home. The vast majority of Ladakhis are villagers, who have, for centuries, provided for most of their physical and emotional needs through interdependent webs of relationship with the land and with community. We remember running through fields as children, picking freely from the orchards of apples and apricots that we came across as we played.

Significant changes took place when Ladakh was opened by the Indian government, first for the army, then for travelers from all around the world. Increasingly, Ladakh was pressured to conform to national development models, and to integrate into the Indian and global economies. Government jobs and tourism offered money-making opportunities and more luxurious lifestyles in Ladakh's capital city, Leh, as well as in bigger Indian towns and cities outside Ladakh. At the same time, the Public Distribution System (PDS) brought in highly subsidized grain, so agriculture quickly became uneconomic.

These changes have strongly influenced the way people think and make a living, over time causing a decline of village and local agriculture, changing diets to depend more on food imports, and increasing the pace of urbanization. As we explore in our recent short film—*Young Farmers in Ladakh*—the implications of these changes for long-term cultural survival, local economic sustainability, and food security are concerning.[1]

Like us, most young people in Ladakh have been trained in English and business and computer sciences, and we do not have the full set of skills our grandparents had—like growing food, making clothes, building houses, and living in community. Our modern "education" presupposes the availability of plentiful employment opportunities in the modern business sector, dependable imports of food from the Indian plains and beyond, and the plausibility of ongoing urbanization and conversion of land from agriculture to buildings and infrastructure.

However, we believe all these assumptions are questionable in the face of existential challenges like global climate change, pandemics, and the massive disruptions to food supply chains caused by lockdowns.

Westernization has come with a lot of glamour and promises of affluence, but today, many younger people are beginning to realize that the chase for modernity and glamour brings little more than dissatisfaction, disconnection, and feelings of addiction.

From deep within us, there is a rising desire to rebuild connection to nature and to other people, and to live in simpler, slower and more meaningful ways. With growing awareness of the problems with the capitalist economic system and western colonialism, many of us have a renewed appreciation of ancient ways.

Now, we are among the growing ranks of young Ladakhis who are returning to Ladakh with the desire to contribute to a new form of progress for the region. Younger people like us do not want Ladakh to become like Delhi or Bangalore. We have seen behind the mirror of industrial modernity, and eschewed consumer values in favor of a commitment to sustainability, justice, health and spiritual wellbeing.

We are realizing the true value of working on the land to grow food —an activity that has been the cornerstone of Ladakhi culture forever. A young farmers' movement is emerging in Ladakh—a movement that we showcase and celebrate in our film.

"Preparing a meal with the vegetables that I picked with my own hands gives me a different level of satisfaction" expresses Tashi Chosgon, a local entrepreneur. "My main motivation to get into farming was to encourage our youngsters and show them the importance of agriculture," explains Sonam Angmo, a pioneer of the young farmers' movement.

In some clear ways, this movement has been strengthened by the pandemic, which highlighted the vital importance of local food systems to our survival. "In these few months, I've realized how important our traditions are ... I can feel a change within me," describes Tsetan Dolma, who runs a local food outlet selling produce and meals from her native village.

Of course, there are still challenges, as there are for young farmers everywhere. The engine of "development" is still pushing strongly to increase tourism and import a corporate consumer culture. But we are encouraged by the enthusiastic reaction to our film at a recent event we organized to discuss these issues. The event featured a screening of the film, a lively panel discussion, a delicious local food lunch provided by a local restaurateur, and a display of local and traditional food products. Perhaps most encouraging was the reception of the agriculture minister, who seems genuinely concerned about the loss of Ladakh's agrarian culture and food sovereignty, and is keen to pursue a food system localization policy agenda.

In one way, Ladakh is luckier than the rest of the world: because globalization happened so fast, the ancient ways are not yet forgotten. At the 2019 Economics of Happiness conference in Ladakh, Keibo Oiwa from Japan lamented the fact that in his country there are few villages to go back to, so relocalization there is much more challenging than in a place like Ladakh.

Here, we still have villages and living ancestral knowledge. Young farmers can learn from their grandparents' traditions, as well as experimenting with new crop varieties and new organic techniques.

That's why we have been organizing agriculture-related workshops for Ladakhi youth, on everything from vermi-composting to mushroom cultivation, and we plan to do more on vegetable gardening, field cultivation, reviving traditional processing techniques, and more. These workshops are a venue for invaluable intergenerational learning.

Through this effort, we hope to step back from the mad rush of modernity, take stock of where we are, and rebuild a local food future based on the wisdom of our traditions.

April 18, 2021

7

FALSE PROMISES

NO MORE "PSEUDO-SOLUTIONS"
Helena Norberg-Hodge

W hen Local Futures first started its global-to-local work in the mid-1970s, there was widespread awareness that both policy change and individual action were needed to solve the world's growing social and ecological problems. In the last two decades, however, mainstream thinking in both the media and academia has focused almost entirely on market solutions rather than political ones. We have been encouraged to see ourselves as consumers instead of citizens and to believe that the best way to effect change is through the decisions we make when we go shopping.

Since we hear so little about the consequences of corporate and government growth-at-any-cost policies, it's easy to believe that the health of the environment depends largely on our willingness to buy recycled paper, install fluorescent light bulbs, and opt for hybrid cars. (Along the way, we are also expected to accept the absurd notion that environmentally friendly products will of course be more costly; that potatoes from the organic farm down the road, for example, will naturally cost more than a packet of potatoes that have been pulverized, reconstituted, frozen, triple-packaged, and shipped to us from a thousand miles away.)

This blind focus on the market is reflected in a giddying array of what I call "pseudo-solutions"—from corporate social responsibility and debt-for-nature swaps to carbon offsets and fair trade. Virtually all these market-based strategies (and there are many more) ignore the fundamental distortions and injustices of the global marketplace. In the name of trade, the marketplace has been steadily deregulated: ever more power has been handed to global traders while health, safety, environmental and labor standards have been systematically gutted. In a world where the value of currencies and commodities is determined by speculation, where the price paid to the producers of coffee or timber or wool very often goes down while the price to the consumer increases, and where hidden subsidies promote environmental breakdown on a colossal scale, it becomes ever more difficult—and expensive—for people to change the world simply by voting through their pocketbooks.

Fundamental critique of the global trading system is perhaps most notably absent in discussions about the relationship between the Global North and South. For centuries, colonialism and debt meant that cheap labor and resources were ruthlessly extracted from the Global South and made available to the wealthier, more industrialized parts of the world. Even though the injustices of the colonial era are widely recognized today, many well-intentioned people argue that we should effectively accelerate that flow by opening more markets in the Global North for products from the Global South. But that step would do little if anything to reduce poverty: long-distance trade primarily benefits a small commercial elite, not poor primary producers in the South.

Failure to understand the workings of the global economy is apparent in other attempts to alleviate poverty. Take micro-credit, for instance. This scheme, which was first introduced into Bangladesh, is spreading around the world like wildfire, and won its creator the Nobel Peace Prize. But not everyone is happy about it. Some months ago, I met Ideh Fesharaki, an Iranian-Canadian researcher who has spent two years studying the effects of micro-credit. She found that it has not succeeded in changing the lives of the poorest of the poor, but it has helped people slightly higher up the socio-economic ladder to "make the leap from the village to the city."

By fueling the migration from rural areas to cities, micro-credit thus contributes to the growth of sprawling Third World cities, in which per capita resource consumption and pollution is vastly higher than in villages, towns, or smaller cities. Every pound of food, the raw materials for every article of clothing, and every bit of construction material comes from elsewhere and must be transported long distances. In a modern concrete high-rise building, there is no space to turn waste into fodder or fertilizer, nor can trees be used for shade or the sun for warmth. And since urbanized populations are exposed to far more advertising pressure, consumption of everything from electricity to soda pop and Barbie dolls increases exponentially. Meanwhile, the women and their families who have been encouraged to abandon the land and communities that provided for them in the past—however imperfectly—

are left increasingly dependent on volatile market forces far beyond their control. The end result is that the pressure on the environment rises dramatically while the vast majority of newly arriving immigrants sees a declining quality of life.

Should we make the best consumer choices we can? Of course. But focusing too much attention on our impact as consumers can blind us to far more strategic steps we can take. If we really want to make a difference, we also need to act politically, in collaboration with others, to insist on different rules in the marketplace. Rather than continuing to promote the creation of a single, deregulated marketplace dominated by giant monopolies, rules are needed that promote instead the flourishing of multiple, truly free markets closer to home. Surely the best way those rules can be monitored and businesses held accountable is if business and capital are rooted, place-based, and localized.

Changing policy is a daunting task, but we can start right now by informing ourselves better on these issues and spreading the word. In this crucial way, education is activism.

May 13, 2010

THE SHARING ECONOMY:
IT TAKES MORE THAN A SMARTPHONE
Steven Gorelick

I ran into my friend Rick the other day in a small town near our homes in northern Vermont. He was just coming out of the book-store, holding a pink plastic bag that, I would soon learn, contained a dozen eggs from his flock of free-range hens. After a bit of small talk, Rick asked, "you don't by any chance have a pair of jumper cables in your car?" I did. "Would you be willing to drive over to the post office and jump my pickup truck? I've been trying to park on hills until I can get a new battery, but there just ain't enough slope at the post office."

After we got his truck started, Rick held out his pink plastic bag and asked, "Could you use some eggs?" As a matter of fact, I could: our elderly hens no longer produce enough for a family of four; Rick's flock, on the other hand, was producing far more than a live-alone bachelor needs. I thanked him for the eggs, and we said our goodbyes.

This exchange—a battery jump for a dozen eggs—wasn't a formal transaction of any kind; it didn't add to GDP, and won't be reported to the IRS. It wasn't even barter, since I would have offered the help without the eggs, and Rick had only brought them to town so he could give them away. But it was an economic exchange nonetheless—one that's so common around here that it hardly rates notice: childcare, garden help, tools, construction labor, and especially food are routinely exchanged, lent or given away without money changing hands. (Last summer someone posted this bulletin board notice: "Free: Take as much as you want. We have two 5-gallon pails of large cukes, 1/2 pail of beans and that much broccoli. I will leave some paper sacks on the porch.") Although this may sound like something that only happens in rural areas, simi-lar exchanges occur in big cities, too—in neighborhoods where people know one another well enough to value their mutual interdependence.

Transactions like these make up what's been called a "gift econ-omy", a topic that anthropologists have studied for almost 100 years.[1] An equally apt term might be "sharing economy"—but that name has already been applied to something that, to my mind at least, is very different.

The "sharing economy" concept first appeared around 2010, launched on a sea of optimism about technology's ability to transform the world for the better. In her TEDx talk describing it, Rachel Botsman, author of *The Rise of Collaborative Consumption*, made liberal use of terms like "revolution" and "seismic shift" to underscore the positive transformations the sharing economy would bring.[2] Exchanges like mine with Rick are okay, she implied, but technology can greatly improve them: "we now live in a global village where we can mimic the ties that used to happen face to face, but on a scale and in a way that has never been possible before." That scaling up, of course, is thanks to the internet, where most collaborative consumption (soon rechristened "the sharing economy") still makes its home.

Botsman's description of how the sharing economy works is fairly straightforward: through online platforms, people who need a product or service can quickly hook up with someone able to provide it. Need to drill a hole? Don't go out and buy an electric drill that "will only be used around 12 to 15 minutes in its entire lifetime"—instead borrow or rent it from someone who already has one. Apply that principle to hundreds of other shareable items and multiply it by millions of sharing events, and we're not only taking steps to eliminate "hyperconsumption" and its environmental impacts, we're creating community as well.

Part of Botsman's thesis makes sense: most modern households contain plenty of infrequently-used tools, gadgets and implements that could easily be shared among many families. This is one of the benefits of co-housing arrangements and ecovillages, in which washing machines, lawnmowers—even fully equipped kitchens—are shared among all the resident households.

But the fact that there are more power drills per capita than necessary misses the essence of hyperconsumption. Thanks to sophisticated marketing campaigns and cradle-to-grave advertising, the consumer culture constantly manufactures new needs; it molds personal identities around brand names, and makes convenience an obsession. Shoppers today can buy robotic vacuum cleaners, forks that monitor their eating habits, and 2-story inflatable cats; they can choose from 504 brands of designer jeans and 6.4 million smartphone apps.[3] These are symptoms of a consumer culture gone mad—and sharing this empty bounty isn't much of a cure.

Perhaps the most profound benefit Botsman claimed for internet-based sharing is that it will enable us "to engage in humanness" again. The sharing economy, she argued, will make us better people, whose "rediscovery of collective good [will] create an economy of 'what's mine is yours.'"

The sharing economy has grown rapidly, but the utopian, egalitarian effects Botsman predicted have failed to materialize: today, in fact, much of the sharing economy looks like big-business-as-usual. Although sometimes defined so broadly that it can include everything from recycling to cooperatives,[4] the sharing economy's standard-bearers are multi-billion dollar corporations: Uber's market capitalization is approximately the same as General Motors, while Airbnb's is 8 times greater than the Hyatt Hotel chain's;[5] Zipcar is now owned by conventional car-rental company Avis, which paid $500 million for it in 2013.[6] These sharing economy companies have more in common with big business than just their market valuations. Uber, for example, is notorious for its ill-treatment of drivers, uses opportunistic "surge-pricing" to inflate fares when demand is high, and is reported to be "a workplace where sexual harassment takes place with impunity."[7] Like other big corporations, these companies use lobbying, PR and campaign contributions to tilt the democratic process in their favor. Uber, for instance, succeeded in quashing New York City's plan to cap the number of cars on the city's streets, while Airbnb was able to scuttle a San Franscisco proposition to limit short-term housing rentals—spending 100 times more than its opponents.[8]

Maybe the profit-oriented businesses at the top aren't saying "what's mine is yours", but what about all those trusting strangers—aren't they rediscovering the collective good? Not so much. A recent survey of sharing economy consumers revealed that "saving money was actually the number one reason for people to participate in the Sharing Economy, with 82% of respondents telling us this was very or somewhat important to them." The *least* important reason? "New relationships/friends or being part of a community."[9]

To be fair, not all sharing economy enterprises are cut from the same cloth as Uber and Airbnb. Tool-lending libraries, for example, are a non-profit means of addressing the electric drill quandary Botsman described. But by their nature, these are local, place-based initiatives: there's a physical space where patrons come to find what they need, and where they'll interact face-to-face with the staff and their own neighbors. Nor are tool-lending libraries an artifact of the internet: the first, in Columbus, Ohio, was founded in 1976, and many others were established in the late 1970s and 80s.[10]

But the sad fact is, digital technologies continue to erode the face-to-face interactions that underpin local economies and communities. It has become a cliché to point out how genuine friendships are being eclipsed by the shallow "friending" that takes place on Facebook, or how people sitting together in a café will stare at their phones rather than engage with each other. If my friend Rick ever decides to carry a smartphone, he might find himself hiring a stranger from TaskRabbit to jump his truck, rather than seeking out a neighbor. With Amazon and other online booksellers dominating the market, the local bookstore where Rick and I met may not be around much longer. These are real-world losses, as more of our social and economic life—including reciprocal exchange—is monetized and absorbed by the internet.

To give the sharing economy its due, I admit that there can be environmental benefits to sharing goods like cars, rather than each of us owning one. But profit-making online platforms like Uber and Lyft aren't the only—or the best—sharing models out there. Many years ago I moved from New York City to a remote valley in the mountains of Colorado. Of all the differences from big city life, none fascinated me more than the fact that everyone in this valley left their vehicles unlocked, with their keys in the ignition. I remarked to one of my new acquaintances how wonderful it was that people were so trusting—so confident that no one would just drive off with their car. He looked puzzled a moment, then smiled and said, "that's not why we leave our keys in the ignition: it's to make sure that if someone needs a car, they'll be able to take it."

Now *that's* a sharing economy.

February 25, 2017

SMALL LOANS, BIG PROBLEMS:
THE FALSE PROMISE OF MICROFINANCE
Helena Norberg-Hodge

E ver since Bill Clinton and the World Bank enthusiastically embraced the microfinance concept in the 1990s, I have been skeptical of its benefits, seeing it as part of a whole package of "market solutions" to our social and environmental crises that, in the long run, make things much worse. These loans often target rural populations who were not previously in debt: they represent the long arm of capitalism reaching into remote rural areas, encouraging a shift away from dependence on the land and the local community, towards competition in a resource-depleting global economy.

It has not been easy to oppose micro-credit: many well-intentioned grassroots activists have bought into the idea that giving "Third World" women loans can eradicate poverty and reduce population growth. This thinking was promoted with missionary zeal, and spread rapidly across the world. In trying to counter it, I have often felt like a heretic. (One of the most difficult moments was when I was asked to debate Muhammad Yunus, the founder of the Grameen Bank, at the height of his popularity, on BBC radio.)

Thank goodness, many people have woken up to the problem. I'm particularly happy to see that my friend and colleague, Jason Hickel, a professor of anthropology at the London School of Economics, has been writing about this issue in the UK *Guardian*. As he says, "microfinance usually makes poverty worse", because the vast majority of microfinance loans are used to fund the purchase of consumer goods that the borrowers simply can't afford: "they end up taking out new loans to repay the old ones, wrapping themselves in layers of debt." Even when used to finance a small business, the most likely outcome is that the new businesses fail, which leads to "vicious cycles of over-indebtedness that drive borrowers even further into poverty." The only winners are the lenders, many of whom charge exorbitant interest rates. Hickel concludes that "microfinance has become a socially acceptable mechanism for extracting wealth and resources from poor people." [1]

I would argue that there are other winners in what Hickel calls "the microfinance game". Corporate interests of all stripes have a vested interest in seeing millions of people drawn more deeply into the debt-based globalized money economy. Interestingly, at the bottom of the webpage where Hickel's article appears there were links to "sponsored content" paid for by the credit card giant Visa, all of them urging more "financial inclusion" in the Global South—in other words, bringing more people into the economic system that corporate interests like Visa dominate. One of the articles, "Helping the world's one billion unbanked women" turns out to be about how "more than 200 million women lack access to a mobile phone, meaning they're excluded from digital banking opportunities." [2] Another article argues that one of the greatest challenges facing policymakers involves "providing some 2.5 billion people with access to formal financial services." [3]

This is propaganda, pure and simple: it is part of a drumbeat coming from think-tanks and corporate-friendly pundits that have been very effective in convincing people—including well-meaning philanthropists and activists—that the solution to global poverty requires pulling ever more people into the global economic system. That system is failing the majority even in the "wealthy" countries, while spurring rampant consumerism and unsustainable resource use worldwide.

The solutions to our many crises—including poverty—will not come from a global marketplace rigged by de-regulatory trade treaties to favor the biggest multinational corporations. Genuine solutions require a halt to further deregulation of global corporations, and shifting towards more localized economies in which people can have real control over their own lives.

June 17, 2015

THINKING OUTSIDE THE GRID
Steven Gorelick

T hirty years ago, a friend of mine published a book called *50 Simple Things You Can Do to Save The Earth*. It described the huge environmental benefits that would result if everyone made some simple adjustments to their way of life. Six hundred thousand gallons of gas could be saved every day, for example, if every commuter car carried just one more passenger; over 500,000 trees could be saved weekly if we all recycled our Sunday newspaper; and so on. The book was immensely popular at the time, at least partly because it was comforting to know we could "save the Earth" so easily.

Unfortunately, the projected benefits of these simple steps were actually insignificant compared to the scale of the problems they addressed. Saving 600,000 gallons of gasoline sounds impressive, but it's only about 0.15% of the amount of fuel consumed in this country daily. Half a million trees every week sounds like a lot too, but the sad fact is that globally, about 35 acres of forest are being lost every minute despite all the newspapers that are now routinely recycled.

50 Simple Things is no longer in print, but the idea that our most urgent environmental problems can be solved by tinkering around the edges of modern life just won't go away. In 2006, for example, Al Gore's *An Inconvenient Truth* DVD included an insert with ten "Things To Do Now" to fight climate change: recycle more, inflate tires to the proper pressure, use less hot water, and other equally "simple things". There are still dozens of websites offering similar tips: 50WaysToHelp.com, for example, has the usual fluff ("don't waste napkins") as well as some suggestions the 1990 book couldn't foresee ("recycle your cellphone", "use e-tickets").[1]

If there's been much of a change in mainstream attitudes to our environmental crises, it's that today's "solutions" rely much more heavily on technology: electric cars and LED light bulbs, clean coal and genetically-engineered biofuels. What this means is that while individuals are still directed towards those same small steps, Big Business will be relied upon for the huge leaps. That was the premise of IBM's "Smarter

Planet" initiative (a corporate campaign implying that our naturally dimwitted planet needs corporate help to avoid embarrassing gaffes like environmental breakdown). Thanks to digital technologies, IBM told us, the Earth is "becoming more intelligent before our eyes—from smarter power grids, to smarter food systems, smarter water, smarter healthcare and smarter traffic systems." [2]

At first glance, *50 Simple Things* and the Smarter Planet initiative are very different, but they share a core assumption, which is that solving our myriad problems won't require systemic change. Instead, it is assumed that modern industrial life can continue its upward and outward expansion forever—smartphones, superhighways, military hardware and all—so long as the public focuses on "simple things" while allowing industry to do whatever might keep us one step ahead of resource depletion and ecological collapse.

This is a dubious strategy at best. Aside from what it means for climate chaos, it ensures that cultural and biological diversity will continue their downward spiral; that the gap between rich and poor will grow even wider; that the wealth and power of transnational corporations will continue to expand. (Needless to say, corporations won't do anything to save the earth if it doesn't add to their bottom line: making the planet more intelligent, for example, was "the overarching framework for IBM's growth strategy.")

In other words, what mainstream environmentalists like Al Gore and corporations like IBM are proposing is just more of the same. For many people this is actually comforting, because systemic change sounds frightening: they are accustomed to their way of life, and fundamental change can seem like stepping off a cliff. But done right, systemic change is something to look forward to, rather than fear. This has already been made abundantly clear by the local food movement, which aims at fundamentally changing the food system. Almost everywhere that local food initiatives have taken root, the result has been more vibrant communities, stronger local economies, better food and a healthier environment. Systemic change via localization simply extends the logic of local food to other basic needs.

Like electric power. Just as we can't know what went into an industrially-grown tomato from Florida or apple from Chile, our continent-wide electric grid prevents us from really knowing the social and environmental costs of flipping on a light switch, using a hair dryer, or making toast in the morning. Did the power come from a nuclear power plant, a huge hydro project in Canada, or a coal-fired plant in the Midwest? Even if we are aware of the costs of these sources of power, few of those costs affect us immediately or directly.

If our electric needs were sourced locally or regionally, on the other hand, we'd have to balance our desire for power with costs that we and our neighbors largely bear ourselves. One can imagine lively debates in communities everywhere about what mix of local power sources—small-scale hydro, wind, biomass, solar—should be employed. Each of these has trade-offs that might be difficult to balance, but most of the costs and benefits would accrue to the same community. If the economic, ecological, and aesthetic costs were too high, many communities would find ways to limit their use of energy—for example by rejecting building permit applications for "McMansions" that use a disproportionate share of the common, limited energy supply.

Ultimately, a greater reliance on local power would eliminate one of the most destructive side-effects of the grid: the misperception that energy is limitless. Grid-connected life leaves us expecting that we should have as much power as we're willing to pay for, 24/7, year in and year out. The angry reaction when the California electric utility PG&E—in an attempt to lower the risk of wildfires—cut power for short periods of time, shows how deeply this expectation has become embedded in the public's consciousness.[3]

Does California's experience mean that people will never accept the limitations of decentralized renewable energy? I believe that such a shift would be far easier than many imagine, based on my own family's experience of living off-the-grid for the past 20 years. Off-grid life doesn't make us environmental heroes: the PV system we rely on for power also has environmental costs, some quite heavy.) The point is only that our attitude towards energy now includes a healthy sense of limits, and that we have quite naturally adjusted our behavior as a result. If the sun hasn't been out for a few days we probably can't run the vacuum cleaner, and we'll have to use a broom instead. If the sun hasn't been out for a week, we'll have to turn off the pump on our deep well, and use the gravity-fed spring instead—which means there won't be enough pressure for showers. In the best of times we don't use electricity to toast bread (anything that turns electricity into heat uses a lot of power); instead we only make toast in the winter, when it can be made on the top of our cookstove.

These and many other adjustments don't feel like sacrifices: they're simple and logical responses to the fact that our source of power is limited and variable. The fuels that power the grid are limited too (as resource depletion and global warming should make clear) but there's no direct link between that fact and the day-to-day experience of grid-connected life.

As the planet heats up and critical resources run low, people will need to adapt in a number of ways. For those of us in the industrialized, over-developed world, one of the most important will be to replace our sense of entitlement with a sense of limits. Our high-consumption lifestyles will be difficult to disengage from—not because they are inescapable products of human nature, but because they are essential to the "growth strategies" of powerful big businesses. The irony is that scaled-down localized alternatives to the media- and advertising-saturated consumer culture would allow the majority to live fuller, richer, more meaningful lives. Nothing to fear, and much to gain.

Systemic change is on no one's list of "simple things": it will require hard work, creativity, and a willingness to stand up to powerful interests. The alternative is to assume that the best we can do is inflate our tires properly and screw in a new light bulb, while allowing the corporate world to continue its quest for limitless power and endless growth, all while destroying the only planet we have.

November 6, 2019

CLIMATE SOLUTIONS:
REAL AND NOT-SO-REAL
Helena Norberg-Hodge

A way from the screens of the mainstream media, the crude "bigger is better" narrative that has dominated economic thinking for centuries is being challenged by a much gentler, more "feminine", inclusive perspective that places human and ecological well-being front and center. People are coming to recognize that *connection*, both to others and to Nature herself, is the wellspring of human happiness. And, every day, new, inspiring initiatives are springing up that offer the potential for genuine prosperity.

At the same time there is a growing awareness—from the grassroots to academia—that the real economy is the natural world, on which we ultimately depend for all our needs. Only when we embrace a structural shift in the current economy—away from dependence on a corporate-run global marketplace, towards diversified local systems—will we be able to live in a way that reflects this understanding.

Tragically, our political and business leaders remain blind to these and other realities. Thanks to the unprecedented influence of global business interests on our national governments, destructive economic policies continue to shape our societies, our cultures and our planet. Even the framing of the climate crisis has been hijacked by the idea that business must continue as usual. In climate negotiations, the $5.3 trillion annual subsidy handed out to the fossil fuel industry goes unmentioned, and, outrageously, emissions from global trade are not even calculated.

Meanwhile the "solutions" to the climate crisis are about adapting to runaway change by employing ever more extractive, centralized technologies. Climate "experts" are convincing us that "sensors and clever algorithms" will be more efficient than farmers in delivering water and synthetic chemicals to crops.

Well-funded think-tanks write about the benefits of automated artificial pollination systems, and release books about architecture in the next century—a world where global temperatures have risen by 7°C and all humans are living in "39 million square kilometers of newly-developed compact megacities near the Earth's poles".[1]

Most of our mainstream thought-leaders fail to imagine a future beyond a highly centralized, corporate-run technocracy. They simply take the dominant system and stretch it to its extremes, overlooking both the extraction of ever increasing quantities of resources and raw materials that such a path will necessitate, and the human and ecological suffering it will cause.

Their vision is profoundly out of touch with socio-economic realities, too. They fail to address the unprecedented wealth inequality that this system has created and continues to exacerbate, and they disregard the effects of mass-displacement on land-based peoples. They envisage a future in which workers will be either totally mobile or replaced by robots, paying lip-service to designated "community-spaces" while ignoring the toll that extreme mobility and mass-unemployment will take on community and personal wellbeing.

In this myopic vision of the future, Big Tech is still held up to be our savior, even though our mega-technological systems have served to separate us from each other and from Nature, while intensifying our global ecological and social crises.

Despite the positive spin given to techno-solutions in the mainstream media, people at the grassroots are not swallowing it. Around the world, hundreds of thousands of people yearn for the deep bonds of community and connection to nature and are quietly sowing the seeds of a very different future.

They are building prosperous local economies and intergenerational communities that provide meaningful, productive work, and reflect our innate desire for love and connection. This is a vision that emerges from a deep experience of what it means to be human.

These efforts demonstrate that real solutions to climate change emanate not from the labs and algorithms of Silicon Valley, but from the enduring wisdoms of land-based cultures, and from the synergetic power of people uniting in community and taking collective action.

The localization movement confronts the climate crisis head-on with three key strategies:

1. **Mitigation:** In the global economy, subsidies, taxes and regulations support the relentless expansion of mega-infrastructure projects, of resource- and chemical-intensive industrial monocultures, and of global trade, which is now *32 times* greater than it was in 1950. It has led us to a crazy situation in which countries are routinely importing and exporting almost identical quantities of identical products, and flying our basic needs around the world for packing and processing before they reach supermarket shelves. Just as wastefully, in the global food system, which demands countless tons of standardized products, 30% or more of harvests are regularly wasted because they do not fit the standardized harvesting, packing and processing machinery. Redirecting economic supports towards building up local systems would cut out this outrageous waste and resource-use, enabling us to reduce fossil fuel use and plastic packaging drastically and immediately. What's more, in contrast to the global marketplace, local markets require a diversity of products, and therefore create incentives for more diversified and ecological production.

2. **Adaptation:** The climate is already changing, and many parts of the world are experiencing alarming water shortages, crop failures and floods. Diversified, local food systems are key in ensuring food security in such uncertain times. In drought-stricken areas of the world, some farmers are transitioning away from thirsty monocrops such as genetically-modified cotton and rice for the global marketplace, and returning to drought-resistant, indigenous seeds (such as millets and local strains of rice). At the same time, farmers producing a diversity of crops for local markets are far more resilient in the face of climate variations and freak weather events, because, unlike their industrial counterparts, they are not completely dependent on a single crop. If one crop fails, they can rely on the many others in cultivation.

3. **Carbon sequestration:** A growing body of research is revealing the key role of healthy soils and healthy ecosystems in drawing carbon out of the atmosphere. They are our most important carbon sinks, offering sequestration potential that far exceeds even the most fantastical technological daydreams. Localization opens up the possibility for the widespread revival of degraded lands, ecosystems and oceans through structurally supporting diversified, genuinely regenerative agriculture, forestry and fishing. By diversifying production, we can eliminate the need for synthetic chemicals and industrial machinery that deplete soils, eliminate biodiversity and poison the environment. We can actually help Mother Nature to renew key ecosystem processes.

Finding solutions to the climate crisis cannot be entrusted to our political and business elite, who are so out of touch with on-the-ground realities that they remain wooed by the empty promises of fast-paced, consumer growth and techno-development. For a healthy future, we need to join those who are forging a very different path forward—one that restores the social and economic structures essential for meeting our needs in ways that nurture the only planet we have.

November 20, 2019

EPILOGUE

BIG PICTURE ACTIVISM
Helena Norberg-Hodge

D espite the countless grassroots projects already under way, the global economic juggernaut can seem too powerful to stop. But because more and more of us are becoming aware of how disastrous the global economy is for people and the planet, I believe that the chances for meaningful change are greater today than ever before.

The environmental costs of the current system have been obvious for quite some time; now the social consequences, too, are becoming more apparent. The gap between rich and poor is escalating to obscene proportions; most people are seeing their real incomes decline, and must work longer hours just to cover basic needs. Governments—many of them too poor to meet their obligations—now respond to the wishes of international lenders rather than their own citizens.

People are beginning to understand that something is fundamentally wrong, and that minor tinkering with the current system is not the answer. A critical mass is ready for fundamental change: what they need is a clear explanation of the root cause of the crises we face, and solutions that are meaningful. Helping to create that critical mass is the goal of what I call "big picture activism".

Raising awareness involves more than just theoretical analysis: every day we can point to inspiring new examples of localization projects. We can show that in North and South, in the city and the country, people are rebuilding connections to others and to Nature, with immediate spiritual, psychological, and practical benefits.

Big picture activism also involves a widespread and holistic re-thinking of basic assumptions. Today's consumer culture is based on myths and misinformation that paralyze and confuse people with contradictory ideas: on the one hand the evening news regularly asks whether consumer spending is adequate to keep the world going; on the other hand we're told that consumer greed is *destroying* the world.

We need to point out that it is not individual greed that created this economic system. None of us voted to put in place an economy that requires endless growth, and uses subsidies, regulations, and our taxes to work against both personal and planetary well-being. Until recently, the broad perspective needed to deconstruct the global economic system has been marginalized, with the field left to narrowly focused market fundamentalists. As a result, it appeared that the only viable option was to head towards ever larger and more inhuman economic scale, with wealth and power concentrated in ever fewer hands. Big picture activism informs us that another way is possible.

For big picture activism to succeed, a number of mental blocks need to be overcome. Many people want to move straight to action when they recognize a problem; they say: *"we already know that the economy's the problem and that corporations have too much power—we don't need to keep discussing that."* But while most of us have a sense that economic forces are behind environmental and social justice problems, few understand how the economy undermines individual and cultural self-esteem; how it exacerbates ethnic, racial, and religious conflict; and how it damages our physical and psychological health. Nor is the majority aware that trade treaties have given corporations and banks so much power that they have become a de facto global government—ruling behind the scenes regardless of whether a "left" or "right" party has been elected. A broad, global-to-local perspective can make even those who already oppose corporate rule more effective.

I also hear people saying, *"the system is going to collapse of its own accord, there's no need to waste time trying to change it."* But despite its deep flaws and contradictions, the economic system may outlive much of the natural and social world. Many years ago, the Swiss economist H.C. Binswanger convinced me that deregulated capital—money de-linked from any standard or limit—could keep multiplying endlessly, even as ecosystems and societies crash. In other words, the economy could keep growing until the last tree falls. A depressing scenario, and one that we must do everything we can to prevent.

Unfortunately, many have completely given up on the idea of fundamentally changing the system. Even committed activists sometimes say: *"there's no point in trying—governments won't listen no matter how many of us march in the streets."* It is true that millions of people marched against the Iraq war, and yet policymakers took us into that senseless and destructive conflict. It is true that millions are opposed to gas frack-ing and nuclear energy, and yet governments continue to promote those technologies. However, the potential for people to really be heard will grow exponentially when they move beyond a fragmented perspective to focus on the common thread that runs through all their concerns. Since the current system is so destructive of both people and the planet, a "new economy" movement—one that is clear about what we are for, not just what we are against—has far greater potential to succeed than almost any single-issue campaign.

There is another stumbling block, one which is particularly common among people whose emphasis is inner transformation. This "New Age" movement has done tremendous good in encouraging millions of people to listen to their hearts and to the wisdom of ancient indig-enous cultures. This deeper consciousness creates a yearning to turn away from the competition and consumerism of the global economy and build more loving relationships with others and the Earth. Until recently, however, there was a tendency in the New Age to focus almost exclusively on the "inner" dimension, on "thinking positively," and personal change. And among those who focused on this inner world, many tended to look down on activists who seemed fixated on the "outer" world.

In the activist community, meanwhile, many have ignored their personal, inner needs, while emphasizing "outer", practical, and politi-cal change. Even though their work is usually born of altruism, ignoring the inner dimension has often hampered their efforts. Neglecting peace of mind and inner reflection and focusing on the negative can lead to self-righteousness and helpless anger. Burnout, conflict, and alienation have often been the consequences. Big picture activism makes clear that our problems have both an inner and an outer dimension, and that solv-ing them requires working on both levels.

Big picture activism does not point a finger at individual politicians, corporations or bankers. Our destructive economic system contin-ues to expand primarily because of ignorance. The economic pundits that promote this growth model have been trained to look at flows of money and numerical representations of the world, and are shielded from many of the real-life social and ecological consequences of their abstract models. The CEOs of large corporations and banks are driven by speculative markets to meet short-term profit and growth targets, and so have even less ability to contemplate the overall impact of their actions. Even concerned consumers, taxpayers and citizens can find it difficult to see the many hidden ways that their choices support an energy-intensive, job- and soul-destroying economy.

The system has been running on blindness for a long time, enabling tremendous destruction to be perpetrated with the best of intentions. The way forward lies not in anger and confrontation, but in actively seeking to encourage peaceful, broad-based, systemic change.

Awareness can spread like fire, and it's empowering to realize that we don't necessarily need to convince our political and economic leaders—who tend to be too locked into their misguided assumptions—or that sector of the population that is deeply immersed in consumerism. Despite enormous financial and time pressures, there is a large number of engaged and concerned people who are working to make the world a better place. They may be focused on improving their children's school, working to protect wildlife, reducing CO_2 emissions, feeding the hungry, or promoting spiritual and ethical values. No matter what problem they're addressing, the economy is a common thread that links them all.

In recent years, many individuals and organizations involved in these separate campaigns have begun to embrace a holistic approach that moves beyond single issues. As a result, a big picture, *broad* analysis is beginning to build a *broad, united* movement. People are harnessing their love, their hope, and their creativity to give birth to a new world—to cultures and economies of happiness.

Excerpted from Local is Our Future: Steps to an Economics of Happiness *(Local Futures 2019).*

REFERENCES

Belonging

1   "Ecotherapy—the green agenda for mental health", *Mind*, 2007.

Globalization and the American Dream

1   "Number of Children & Adolescents Taking Psychiatric Drugs in the U.S.", CCHR International, April 2018.
2   "Eating Disorders Current Trends", National Association of Social Workers, June 30, 2005; Favaro, A., et al, "Time trends in age at onset of anorexia nervosa and bulimia nervosa", Journal of Clinical Psychiatry Vol 70 (12), Dec 2009. pp. 1715-21.
3   "United States School Shootings, 1990-present", BallotPedia, Sept 28, 2018; Rosenblatt, Roger, "The Killing of Kayla", *Time*, March 5, 2000.
4   "Suicide Among Youth", Centers for Disease Control, September 15, 2017.
5   Chalabi, Mona, "How Many Times Does the Average Person Move?" FiveThirtyEight, January 29, 2015.
6   Schabner, Dean, "Americans Work More Than Anyone", ABC News, May 1, 2018; Nicolaci da Costa, Pedro, "More Americans Need a 2nd Job to Make Ends Meet", ABC News, August 8, 2017.
7   Brody, Jane, "Screen Addiction is Taking a Toll on Children", *New York Times*, July 6, 2015; Gunn, Jennifer, "Get Outside! The Outdoor Education Movement Takes Root", Room 241, Concordia University - Portland, June 28, 2018.
8   "New 2015 Stats: Face of Plastic Surgery Goes Younger Due to Growing Social Media and Reality TV Influence on Millennials", American Academy of Facial Plastic Surgery and Reconstructive Surgery, January 14, 2016.
9   Prolongeau, Hubert, "India's skin-whitening creams highlight a complex over darker complexions", *The Guardian*, July 24, 2015.
10 "Income and Poverty in the United States: 2016", US Census Bureau, September 12, 2017.
11 "An Economy for the 99%", Oxfam International, January 16, 2017; "An Economy for the 1%", Oxfam International, January 18, 2016.
12 Diamond, Jared, "What's Your Consumption Factor?" *New York Times*, January 2, 2008.

Costs of the Great Acceleration

1   Steffen, W., Broadgate, W., Deutsch, L., Gaffney, O., and Ludwig, C. "The trajectory of the Anthropocene: The Great Acceleration", The Anthropocene Review, 16 January, 2015.

2   Stockholm Resilience Centre, "New Planetary Dashboard Shows Increasing Human Impact", http://www.stockholmresilience.org/research/research-news/2015-01-15-new-planetary-dashboard-shows-increasing-human-impact.html.

3   Giljum, S., Dittrich, M., Lieber, M., and Lutter, S. (2014) "Global Patterns of Material Flows and their Socio-Economic and Environmental Implications: A MFA Study on All Countries World-Wide from 1980 to 2009", Resources 3, 319-339.

4   Dobbs, R., Oppenheim, J., Thompson, F., Brinkman, M., and Zornes, M. (2011) "Resource Revolution: Meeting the world's energy, materials, food, and water needs", McKinsey Global Institute.

5   Worldwatch, 2015.

6   Jowit, J. "Global hunger for plastic packaging leaves waste solution a long way off", The Guardian, December 29, 2011.

7   Norris, J., "Make Them Eat Cake: How America is Exporting Its Obesity Epidemic", Foreign Policy, September 3, 2013.

8   GRAIN, "Hungry for Land: Small farmers feed the world with less than a quarter of all farmland", 28 May, 2014.

9   American Geophysical Union, "Worldwide ship traffic up 300 percent since 1992", ScienceDaily, November 17, 2014.

10 Scutt, D., "This chart shows an insane forecast for worldwide growth of ships, cars, and people", Business Insider Australia, April 19, 2016.

11 Hoornweg, D., and Bhada-Tata, P. (2012) "What a waste? A global review of solid waste management", Urban development series knowledge papers; no. 15, Washington, DC: World Bank Group.

12 http://www.makeinindia.com/.

13 Oxfam, "An economy for the 1%", Oxfam Briefing Paper 210, January 18, 2016.

14 Monbiot, G., "One Rolex Short of Contentment", The Guardian, December 10, 2013.

Globalization Produces Sushi... and Slavery

1   International Labour Organisation, "Forced labour, modern slavery and human trafficking", https://www.ilo.org/global/topics/forced-labour/lang--en/index.htm.

2   U.S. Department of State, Trafficking in Persons Report, "Heroes: Van-nak Anan Prum, Cambodia, Class of 2012", http://www.tipheroes.org/vannak-anan-prum/.

Supply Chain Failures

1   U.S. Bureau of Labor Statistics, Economic News Release, Consumer Price Index Summary, April 2022.
2   Bizouati-Kennedy, Yaël, "Global Food Prices Hit Record High in March", Yahoo! Finance, April 8, 2022.
3   Eccles, Louise, "Will a chicken fillet soon be pricier than a filet mignon?" The Times (London), May 1, 2022.
4   Swanson, Ana, "Governments tighten grip on global food stocks, sending prices higher", New York Times, April 30, 2022.
5   World Trade Organization, "Evolution of trade under the WTO: handy statistics", WTO.org.
6   Cook, Rob, "U.S. Beef Imports vs. Exports by Year", NationalBeefWire.com, September 10, 2022.
7   Observatory of Economic Complexity (OEC), OEC Profiles: Butter, https://oec.world/en/profile/hs/butter.
8   Workman, Daniel, "World's Top Exports: Fresh or Frozen Beef Imports by Country" and "World's Top Imports: Fresh or Frozen Beef Exports by Country", WorldsTopExports.com.
9   GRAIN, "Food and climate: the forgotten link", GRAIN.org, September 28, 2011.
10 Anderson, Sarah and Cavanaugh, John, "The Top 200: the Rise of Corporate Power", Institute for Policy Studies, December 4, 2000.

Globalization and Terror

1   Based on personal experience. For additional information, see for example Mathew, Joseph C, Ethnic Conflict in Bhutan (Nirala Publications, 1999); Mørch, Maximillian, "Bhutan's Dark Secret: The Lhotshampa Expulsion", The Diplomat, Sept 21, 2016.
2   Chossudovsky, Michel, The Globalization of Poverty: Impacts of IMF and World Bank Reforms (London: Third World Network, Penang and Zed Books, 1997). Chapter 13.
3   Smith, Helena, "Neo-fascist Greek party takes third place in wave of voter fury", The Guardian, September 20, 2015.

How Globalization Leads to Authoritarianism

1   Faux, Jeff, "NAFTA's Impact on U.S. Workers", Economic Policy Institute, Working Economics Blog, December 9, 2013.
2   Ibid.
3   Hart-Landsberg, M., "Trump's Economic Policies Are No Answer to Our Problems", *Reports from the Economic Front*, February 13, 2017.
4   Ibid.
5   Moberg, D., "The China Syndrome", *In These Times*, April 9, 2004.
6   Friends of the Earth UK, "How to ... oppose a supermarket planning application: a short guide", September 2005.
7   Laveccia, Olivia and Mitchell, Stacy, "Amazon's Stranglehold: How the Company's Tightening Grip Is Stifling Competition, Eroding Jobs, and Threatening Communities", Institute for Local Self-Reliance, November, 2016.
8   Sales Tax Institute, "State Sales Tax Rates", July 1, 2017. http://www.salestaxinstitute.com/resources/rates.
9   Corporate Europe Observatory/ Council of Canadians/ Transnational Institute (2013) *The right to say no: EU- Canada trade agreement threatens fracking bans*, http://corporateeurope.org/publications/right-say-no-eu-canada-trade- agreement-threatens-fracking-bans.
10 Friends of the Earth Europe, "The TTIP of the anti-democracy iceberg", *Friends of the Earth Europe Report*, October, 2013.
11 Atran, Scott, speech: "Youth need values and dreams"—address to the UN assembly, April 23, 2015, https://www.youtube.com/watch?v=qlbirlSA-dc.
12 Smith-Spark, Laura, "A far-right extremist killed 77 people in Norway...", CNN, July 23, 2021.

Human Nature: Cause or Cure?

1   The Social Dilemma, https://vimeo.com/462049229.
2   Golding, William, The Lord of the Flies, Faber and Faber, 1954.
3   Bregman, Rutger, Humankind: A Hopeful History, translated by Elizabeth Manton and Erica Moore, Back Bay Books, 2019.

March of the Monoculture

1   Cited in Bodley, John H, *Victims of Progress* (Rowman & Littlefield, 2014). p. 153.

2   Ibid, p. 112.
3   Ibid, p. 129.
4   Ibid, p. 11.

What is Education For?

1   Cited in Goldsmith, Edward, *The Way* (Boston: Shambala, 1993), p. 282.
2   Berry, Wendell, *The Unsettling of America* (San Francisco: Sierra Club, 1977), p. 147.
3   Norberg-Hodge, Helena, *Ancient Futures: Learning from Ladakh* (San Francisco: Sierra Club, 1991), pp. 110-111.
4   Ibid.
5   Gatto, John Taylor, "A Map, A Mirror, and A Wristwatch", *Challenging the Giant* (Albany, NY: Down to Earth Books, 1996), p. 321.
6   Orr, David, *Earth in Mind* (Washington, DC: Island Press, 1994), p. 31.
7   Cited in Sheldrake, Rupert, *The Rebirth of Nature* (Rochester, VT: Park Street Press), p. 40.
8   *Scientific American,* Sept. 1989.
9   Goldsmith, Edward, op. cit., p. xiv.
10   Ibid., p. xv.
11   Nordhaus, William, "Greenhouse Economics: Count Before You Leap", *The Economist*, July 7, 1990, cited in Douthwaite, Richard, *The Growth Illusion*, op. cit., p. 199.
12   *New York Times* magazine, Dec. 1, 1996, p. 40.
13   Orr, David, op. cit., pp. 32-3.
14   "Monsanto Environmental Annual Review, 1995", Monsanto Environmental Public Affairs (800 North Lindbergh Blvd., St. Louis, MO 63167), p. 20.
15   Although underwritten by the Monsanto and Pioneer corporations, the book was published under the auspices of the National 4-H Council, 7100 Connecticut Ave., Chevy Chase, MD 20815.
16   Jacobson, Michael F. and Mazur, Laurie Ann, *Marketing Madness* (Boulder, CO: Westview Press, 1995), p. 33.
17   "Farewell Europe", *New Scientist*, Nov. 9, 1996, p. 11.
18   Reported on Today programme, Radio 4, England, May 30, 1997.
19   Soley, Lawrence C., *Leasing the Ivory Tower: The Corporate Takeover of Academia* (Boston: South End, 1995), p. 71.
20   Rampe, David, "The BankAmerica Dean", *New York Times*, July 19, 1998.
21   "Testing times for Britain's Students", *London Times*, Feb. 19, 1997, p. 15.

22 Stead, Deborah, op. cit., p. 30.
23 Ibid.
24 Jacobson, Michael F. and Mazur, Laurie Ann, op. cit., p. 34.
25 Ibid., p. 31.
26 Ibid., p. 32.
27 Cushman, John, "Critics Rise up Against Environmental Education", *New York Times*, Apr. 22, 1997.
28 Gatto, John Taylor, "On the Scientific Management of Children", op. cit., pp. 40-41.
29 Ibid., p. 42.

Groomed to Consume

1 "Children, Adolescents, and Advertising", *Journal of the American Academy of Pediatrics*, vol. 118, number 6.
2 "The State of Consumption Today", Worldwatch Institute.
3 Schor, Juliet B., *"Born to Buy: The Commercialized Child and the New Consumer Culture"* (Scribner, New York: 2004).
4 Goldfarb, Z. and Boorstein, Michelle, "Pope Francis denounces 'trickle-down' economic theories in critique of inequality". *The Washington Post*. November 26, 2013.

Our Obsolescent Economy

1 Municipal Solid Waste, EPA Report on the Environment, 2017; "Municipal Solid Waste Factsheet", Center for Sustainable Systems, University of Michigan, 2018, Pub. No. CSS04-15.
2 Chen, Angus, "The Continent that Contributes the Most to E-Waste is..." National Public Radio, January 26, 2017.
3 "Irreparable Damage", *Washington Times*, Jan 9, 2007.
4 Morris, Natalie, "Fewer shoe repair shops mean business for those remaining", *The State Journal-Register*, March 5, 2012; "Shoe Repair in the US: Market Research Report", IBIS World, Apr 2017.
5 Ewen, Stuart, *Captains of Consciousness: Advertising and the Social Roots of the Consumer Culture* (New York: McGraw-Hill, 1976).
6 London, Bernard, "Ending the Depression Through Planned Obsolescence", 1932.
7 Ibid.
8 *Pyramids of Waste: The Light Bulb Conspiracy*, 2010, a documentary film by Cosima Dannoritzer. Viewed at FilmsforAction.org.
9 Seinfeld, "The Seven", episode 13, season 7. Aired February 1, 1996.

10 Walton, Andy, "Life Expectancy of a Smartphone", *Houston Chronicle.* Accessed Oct 15, 2018.

11 Ibid.

12 Beres, Damon, and Campbell, Andy, "Apple is Fighting a Secret War to Keep You from Repairing Your Phone", Huffington Post, June 9, 2016.

13 Solon, Olivia, "A Right to Repair: Why Nebraska Farmers are Taking on John Deere and Apple", *The Guardian*, March 6, 2017; Beres, Damon, "Big Tech Squashes New York's "Right to Repair" Bill", Huffington Post, June 17, 2016.

14 "About Repair Café", repaircafe.org/en/about.

The Global Economy's "Impeccable Logic"

1 Piketty, Thomas, *Capital in the Twenty-first Century*, English-language edition, (Cambridge: Harvard University Press, 2014).

2 Oxfam, "Time to Care", Report Summary, January 2020; "Inequality Kills", Report Summary, January 2022.

3 Tapscott, Don, Huffington Post, "Extreme Disparity of Wealth Dominates Davos", January 28, 2014.

4 "How Should we Distribute Our Wealth", NPR, TED Radio Hour, February 6, 2015.

5 http://en.wikipedia.org/wiki/Summers_memo.

6 Ibid.

7 Ibid.

8 http://en.wikipedia.org/wiki/Lawrence_Summers.

9 http://www.whirledbank.org/ourwords/summers.html.

The Super Bowl of Subsidies

1 Epstein, Jacob, "How the NFL makes money", Investopedia, January 27, 2022; "Total revenue of all NFL teams from 2001 to 2020", Statista, https://www.statista.com/statistics/193457/total-league-revenue-of-the-nfl-since-2005/.

2 CNN Business, "NFL gets billions in subsidies from U.S. taxpayers", January 30, 2015.

3 Doyle, Patrick "Why is the NFL a non-profit?", Public Source, October 9, 2014 (updated April 28, 2015) https://www.publicsource.org/why-is-the-nfl-a-nonprofit/.

4 Coady, David, Parry, Ian, Le, Nghia-Piotr, Shang, Baoping, "Global Fossil Fuel Subsidies Remain Large: An Update Based on Country-Level Estimates", IMF Working Paper No. 19/89, May 2, 2019.

5   "Toxic Air: the Price of Fossil Fuels", Greenpeace, February 2020.
6   Sumaila, U., Rashid, et al, "Updated estimates and analysis of global fisheries subsidies", *Marine Policy*, Volume 109, November 2019.
7   Farm Subsidies, Free Trade, and the Doha Round, Heritage Foundation, February 5, 2007.
8   National Sustainable Agriculture Coalition, "Organic Agriculture Research & Extension Initiative"; Congressional Research Service, "Federal Research and Development (R&D) Funding: FY2022".

Putting Technology in its Place

1   Heffernan, Olive, "Seabed mining is coming – bringing mineral riches and fears of epic extinctions", *Nature*, July 24, 2019.
2   "'Tsunami of data could consume one-fifth of global electricity by 2025", *The Guardian*, December 11, 2017.

Resisting the Technocratic Paradigm

1   "Encyclical Letter Laudato Si' of the Holy Father Francis on Care for our Common Home", https://www.vatican.va/content/francesco/en/encyclicals/documents/papa-francesco_20150524_enciclica-laudato-si.html.

Branding Tradition:
A Bittersweet Tale of Corporate Capitalism

1   Egan, Hannah Palmer, "Sweet Deal: A Giant Sugaring Operation Banks on Maple", *Seven Days*, March 25, 2015.
2   Brown, Josh, University of Vermont, UVM Today, "Remaking Maple", November 6, 2014.

Technology and its Discontents

1   Mander, Jerry, *In the Absence of the Sacred* (Sierra Club: San Francisco, 1991).
2   Speech at University of Illinois Urbana-Champaign, Feb. 24, 2004.
3   Gates, Bill, "Here's my plan to improve our world—and how you can help", *Wired magazine*, November 12, 2013.
4   https://www.quotemaster.org/author/Mark+Zuckerberg.
5   Konnikova, Maria, "Is Internet Addiction a Real Thing?" *The New Yorker*, November 26, 2014.

6   Campbell, Dennis, "Facebook and Twitter 'harm young people's mental health'", *The Guardian*, May 19, 2017.

7   "Teen suicide rate suddenly rises with heavy use of smartphones, social media," *Washington Times*, Nov. 14, 2017.

8   Solon, Olivia, "Ex-Facebook president Sean Parker: site made to exploit human 'vulnerability'", *The Guardian*, November 9, 2017.

9   Lewis, Paul, "'Our minds can be hijacked': the tech insiders who fear a smartphone dystopia", *The Guardian*, October 6, 2017.

10   Wong, Julia Carrie, "Former Facebook executive: social media is ripping society apart", *The Guardian*, December 12, 2017.

11   Lewis, P. op. cit.

12   Carr, Nicholas, *The Shallows: What the Internet Is Doing to Our Brains* (W.W. Norton, 2010).

13   Wong, Julia Carrie, op. cit.

14   Lewis, P. op. cit.

15   Kircher, Madison Malone, "Facebook Releases App for Kids Under 13. What Could Possibly Go Wrong Here?" *New York Magazine*, December 4, 2017.

16   "'Tsunami of data' could consume one-fifth of global electricity by 2025", *The Guardian*, December 11, 2017.

The Folly of Farm-Free Food

1   Monbiot, G. "Meet the ecomodernists: ignorant of history and paradoxically old-fashioned", *The Guardian*, 24 September, 2015.

2   Monbiot, G., "Lab-grown food will soon destroy farming—and save the planet", *The Guardian*, 8 January, 2020.

3   Smaje, C., "Of chancers and last-chancers", Small Farm Future blog, 12 January, 2020. https://smallfarmfuture.org.uk/2020/01/of-chancers-and-last-chancers/.

4   GRAIN and IATP, "Emissions impossible: How big meat and dairy are heating up the planet", GRAIN and the Institute for Agriculture and Trade Policy (IATP), 18 July, 2018.

5   Stanley, P.L. et al., "Impacts of soil carbon sequestration on life cycle greenhouse gas emissions in Midwestern USA beef finishing", *Agricultural Systems*, Volume 162, May 2018.

6   Balmford, A. et al., "The environmental costs and benefits of high-yield farming", *Nature Sustainability* 1, 2018.

7   Kroll, A. and Schulman, J., "Leaked Documents Reveal the Secret Finances of a Pro-Industry Science Group", *Mother Jones*, 28 October, 2013.

8   American Council on Science and Health, "Conventional Farms Are Better for Environment Than Organic Farms", 22 September, 2018.

9   Fish J., "To all editors, reviewers and authors: time to move on regarding land sparing", *Ideas for Sustainability*, 8 October, 2015.

10   Pearce, F., "Sparing vs Sharing: The Great Debate Over How to Protect Nature", *Yale Environment* 360, 3 December, 2018.

11   Kremen, C., "Reframing the land-sparing/land-sharing debate for bio-diversity conservation", *Annals of the New York Academy of Sciences* Vol. 1355, 2015; and Kremen, C. and Miles, A., "Ecosystem Services in Biologically Diversified versus Conventional Farming Systems: Benefits, Externalities, and Trade-Offs", *Ecology and Society* 17(4), 2012.

12   Perfecto, I., Vandermeer, J. and Wright, A., *Nature's Matrix: Linking Agriculture, Biodiversity Conservation and Food Sovereignty*, 2nd Edition, London: Routledge, 2019.

13   See for example: Chappell, M.J. and LaValle, L.A. (2011) "Food security and biodiversity: can we have both? An agroecological analysis", Agriculture and Human Values 28; Tuck, S.L. et al. (2014) "Land use intensity and the effects of organic farming on biodiversity: a hierarchical meta-analysis", Journal of Applied Ecology 51(3); Barthel, S., Crumley, C. and Svedin, U. (2013) "Bio-cultural refugia—Safeguarding diversity of practices for food security and biodiversity", Global Environmental Change 23 (5); Kremen, C. and Miles, A. (2012) "Ecosystem Services in Biologically Diversified versus Conventional Farming Systems: Benefits, Externalities, and Trade-Offs", Ecology and Society 17(4); and Pimbert, M.P. (2018) *Food Sovereignty, Agroecology and Biocultural Diversity*, London: Routledge.

14   GRAIN, "Hungry for land: small farmers feed the world with less than a quarter of all farmland", GRAIN 28 May, 2018.

15   Netting, R. McC., *Smallholders, Householders: Farm Families and the Ecology of Intensive, Sustainable Agriculture*, Redwood City, CA: Stanford University Press, 1993.

16   See also, Kalt, T., "The Myth of the Green City: Mapping the Uneven Geographies of E-Mobility", in Vormann, B. and Lammert, C. (eds.) *Contours of the Illiberal State: Governing Circulation in the Smart Economy, Chicago*, IL: University of Chicago Press, 2019; and Hornborg, A., "A globalised solar-powered future is wholly unrealistic—and our economy is the reason why", The Conversation, 6 September, 2019. https://theconversation.com/a-globalised-solar-powered-future-is-wholly-unrealistic-and-our-economy-is-the-reason-why-118927.

17   Architecture 2030, "Why the Building Sector?" https://architecture2030.org/buildings_problem_why/.

18   Watts, J., "Concrete: the most destructive material on Earth", *The Guardian*, 25 February, 2019.

19   Srivastava, M. and Gopal, P., "What's holding India back? Business is battling farmers over land, putting $98 bn in investments, and an industrial revolution, on hold", *The Economic Times*, 10 October, 2009; and Chauduri, P.P., "Bright lights, dim policy: Farm policies hinder the movement of rural Indians to cities. This undermines their progress", *Hindustan Times*, 2 June, 2009.

20   Fitzgerald, D., *Every Farm a Factory: The Industrial Ideal in American Agriculture*, New Haven, CT: Yale University Press, 2010.

21   Hoornweg, D., Bhada-Tata, P., and Kennedy, C., "Environment: Waste production must peak this century", *Nature* 502(7473), 30 October, 2013.

22   Biello, D., "City Dwellers Drive Deforestation in 21st Century", *Scientific American*, 8 February, 2010.

23   Moran, D. and Kanemoto, K., "Identifying species threat hotspots from global supply chains", *Nature Ecology & Evolution* 1, 4 January, 2017.

24   Monbiot, G., "The age of loneliness is killing us", The Guardian, 14 October, 2014; Monbiot, G., "Neoliberalism is creating loneliness. That's what's wrenching society apart", *The Guardian*, 12 October, 2016; Bond, M., "The hidden ways that architecture affects how you feel", BBC Future, 5 June, 2017.

25   Geher, G., "The Urbanization-Mental Health Connection: Three evolution-based reasons that humans were shaped for small-scale living", *Psychology Today*, 28 August, 2016.

26   Monbiot, G., "The town that's found a potent cure for illness—community", *The Guardian*, 21 February, 2018.

27   Netting, R. McC (1993) op cit.

28   Miller, D., "How dirt heals us", *Yes Magazine*, 7 December, 2013.

29   Feldmar, J., "Gardening could be the hobby that helps you live to 100", BBC Worklife, 10 December, 2018; Pretty, J.N. et al, "Green Mind Theory: How Brain-Body Behaviour Links into Natural and Social Environments for Healthy Habits", *International Journal of Environmental Research and Public Health* 14, 2017.

30   E.g. Monbiot, G., "Housebroken", George Monbiot blog, 19 November, 2012. https://www.monbiot.com/2012/11/19/housebroken/; and "Why we couldn't care less about the natural world", *The Guardian*, 9 May, 2014.

31   Monbiot, G., "The problem with education? Children aren't feral enough", *The Guardian*, 7 October, 2013.

32   Williams, F., The Nature Fix: *Why Nature Makes Us Happier, Healthier, and More Creative*, New York: W.W. Norton, 2017.

33   Smaje, C. (2020) op cit.

34 Berry, W. "Farmland Without Farmers", *The Atlantic*, 19 March, 2015.
35 Netting, op cit.
36 Ries, C., "A Green New Deal Must Prioritize Regenerative Agriculture", Truthout.org, 9 May, 2019; Heinberg, R., "Fifty Million Farmers", Resilience.org, 17 November, 2006.

Resist Globally, Renew Locally

1 Harris, John, "How to take over your town: the inside story of a local revolution", *The Guardian*, June 12, 2019.

What to Do When the World is on Fire

1 Begley, Sarah, "The Future of Food: Experts Predict How Our Plates Will Change", *Time magazine*, October 4, 2014.
2 Spero Rn, David, "Pioneer Days are Over: It's time to become natives to this land", AnInjusticeMag.com, May 6, 2021; Lucchesi, Nick, "Elon Musk says we need to build more tunnels", Inverse.com, January 30, 2016.
3 Plotnikova, Sasha, "Designing for a world after climate catastrophe", UnevenEarth.org, October 22, 2019.
4 Kaufman, Mark, "World's carbon emissions grew in 2019 to their highest levels ever", Mashable.com, December 3, 2019; Carrington, Damian, "World's consumption of materials hits record 100bn tonnes a year", *The Guardian*, January 22, 2020.
5 "Water contamination fears from bushfire flame retardant", 9News.com, January 14, 2020.
6 National Farm Worker Ministry, "Modern-Day Slavery", https://nfwm.org/farm-workers/farm-worker-issues/modern-day-slavery/.
7 Cummins, Ronnie, "The 9% lie: industrial agriculture and climate change", Regeneration International, July 29, 2019.
8 Rodale Institute White Paper, "Regenerative Organic Agriculture and Climate Change", [no date].
9 Monbiot, George, "Small is Bountiful", www.monbiot.com, June 10, 2008.
10 Savory, Allan, "How to fight desertification and reverse climate change", TED talk 2013.
11 de Oliveira, Inez, "Ernst Götsch: the creator of the real green revolution", BelieveEarth, [no date].
12 Gourlay, Colin, et al, "How extreme conditions drove Australia's record

bushfire disaster", ABC.net.au, February 23, 2020; Deacon, Ben, "Californian fires are mirroring Australia's Black Summer, experts say, driven by record drought and heat", ABC.net.au, September 17, 2020.

13 Cagle, Susie, "'Fire is medicine': the tribes burning California forests to save them", *The Guardian*, November 21, 2019.

14 Marciniak, Catherine, "The Community Defenders helping to save a Gondwana rainforest from bushfire", ABC.net.au, December 9, 2019.

The Great Deceleration

1 https://candecreix.degrowth.net/.

2 Gudynas, E., "Buen Vivir: Today's Tomorrow", *Development* 54(4) 2011

3 cf. Marti, N. and Pimbert, M.,"Barter Markets: Sustaining people and nature in the Andes", IIED. http://pubs.iied.org/14518IIED/, and Argumedo, A. and Pimbert, M., "Bypassing Globalization: Barter markets as a new indigenous economy in Peru", Development 53(3), 2010.

4 Fitzgerald, D., Every *Farm a Factory: The Industrial Ideal in American Agriculture*, New Haven CT: Yale University Press, 2003.

Educating for a New Economy

1 Cubberly, E.P., *Public Education in the United States* (Boston: Houghton Mifflin, 1934), cited in Reich, Robert B., *The Work of Nations* (New York: Alfred A. Knopf, 1991), p. 60.

2 "Leanne Simpson and Glen Coulthard on Dechinta Bush University, Indigenous land-based education and embodied resurgence", Decolonization: Indigeneity, Education and Society, November 26, 2014, https://decolonization.wordpress.com/2014/11/26/leanne-simpson-and-glen-coulthard-on-dechinta-bush-university-indigenous-land-based-education-and-embodied-resurgence/.

From Global to Local in India

1 Shiva, Vandana, "India Needs Her Small Farmers", Countercurrents, April 30, 2007.

2 See Alliance for Sustainable & Holistic Agriculture (ASHA), www.kisanswaraj.in.

3 See IndiaGMInfo.org.

4 See IndiaFDIWatch.org.

5 See vikalpsangam.org.

Tosepan: Resistance and Renewal in Mexico

1 "Free Trade and Mexico's Junk Food Epidemic", GRAIN, March 2, 2015.

2 Wise, Timothy A., "Policy Space for Mexican Maize: Protecting Agro-bio-diversity by Promoting Rural Livelihoods", Global Development and Environment Institute, Tufts University, February 2007; Weisbrot, Mark, et al, "Did NAFTA Help Mexico? An Update After 23 Years", Center for Economic and Policy Research, March 2017.

3 GRAIN, op. cit.; Clark, Sarah E., et al., "Exporting obesity: US farm and trade policy and the transformation of the Mexican consumer food environment", *International Journal of Occupational and Environmental Health*, 2012, 18:1, 53-64.

4 "Mexico's Extreme Inequality: 1% Owns Half of Country's Wealth", Tele-Sur, June 25, 2015.

5 "Investigadores de la UNAM, revelan más de 500 conflictos ambientales en México y construye mapa que los georeferencia y categoriza", *México Ambiental*, March 16, 2018.

6 "At What Cost? Irresponsible business and the murder of land and environmental defenders", Global Witness, 2018.

7 Bonfil Batalla, Guillermo, *México Profundo: Reclaiming a Civilization* (Austin: University of Texas), 1996.

8 "Hidroeléctrica Puebla 1, Puebla, Mexico", Environmental Justice Atlas, February 1, 2017.

9 "Walmart Store in Cuetzalan, Puebla, Mexico", Environmental Justice Atlas, March 3, 2017.

10 Gonzalez Amádor, Roberto, "Cuetzalan frenó a Wal-Mart; se impuso la economía real", *La Jornada*, April 25, 2012.

11 Barstow, David, "Wal-Mart Hushed Up a Vast Mexican Bribery Case", *New York Times*, April 21, 2012.

12 See "Tosepantomin", Unión de Cooperativas Tosepan, 2016; Bien, Ethan, "'Light for everyone': Indigenous youth mount a solar-powered resistance", Mongabay, December 10, 2018.; "Comunidad indígena recurre a energía alternativa, rechazan a CFE", Slow Food, January 20, 2017; "Yolseuiloyan: Donde el Corazón descansa y se fortalece", Unión de Cooperativas Tosepan, 2018.

13 Albores, María Luisa, "Experiencia de Agroecología en la Tosepan...", *La Jornada del Campo*, December 17, 2016.

14 Bien, Ethan, "An Indigenous Cooperative is Dodging Bullets to Defend Their Land", *In These Times*, June 21, 2018.

The Case for Local Food

1   Worldwatch Institute, "Globetrotting Food Will Travel Farther Than Ever This Thanksgiving", CropChoice.com, http://cropchoice.com/leadstry-4fe2.html.

2   Beef and potatoes are two examples of commodities for which the quantities imported and exported annually are consistently nearly identical. See these official statistics for more information on various crops: "Data: U.S. Export share of Production, Import Share of Consumption (2008-2014)", United States Department of Agriculture Economic Research Service, Jan 25, 2018.

3   Plumer, Brad, "How GMO crops conquered the United States", *Vox Media*, Aug 12, 2014.

4   United States Department of Agriculture, "Census of Agriculture: 2007 Census Publications".

7 Billion for Dinner? Here's How to Feed Them

1   FAO, IFAD, UNICEF, WFP and WHO, "The State of Food Security and Nutrition in the World 2018: Building climate resilience for food security and nutrition", Rome, FAO, 2018.

2   World Food Prize Foundation, "Laureates, 2013 - Van Montagu, Chilton, Fraley", https://www.worldfoodprize.org/en/laureates/20102019_laureates/2013_van_montagu_chilton_fraley/.

3   World Food Prize Foundation, "Sponsors". This page has been removed from the World Prize Foundation website, but it has been archived at https://web.archive.org/web/20211205054030/https://www.worldfoodprize.org/en/about_the_foundation/sponsors/.

4   Rosset, Peter, "The multiple functions and benefits of small farm agriculture in the context of global trade negotiations," *Institute for Food and Development Policy*, Food First Policy Brief No. 4, Sept 1999. See also: "'Agroecology outperforms large-scale industrial farming for global food security' says UN expert", *United Nations Human Rights Office of the High Commissioner*, June 22, 2010; "Industrial Agriculture and Small-scale Farming", GlobalAgriculture.org; Badgely, Catherine, et al., "Organic agriculture and the global food supply", Renewable Agriculture and Food Systems Vol 22 (2), June 2007; Pretty, J. N., et al., "Resource-conserving agriculture increases yields in developing countries", *Environmental Science and Technology* Vol 40 (4), 2006.

5   Williamson, Jeff, Sargent, Steve, and Olmstead, Jim, "Preliminary Stud-

ies of Mechanically Harvested Blueberries for Fresh Markets in Florida", University of Florida, Gainesville.

6   As one blueberry grower put it, "When you go out in the field and you watch a machine pick, if you're not used to it the first time, it looks like you're dropping a lot on the ground. But if you weigh the cost of picking by hand against what you're losing, it's way better to pick by machine." Jeffries, Anne-Marie, "Mechanical Blueberry Harvesting Can Save On Labor", GrowingProduce.com, March 4, 2010.

7   Berry, Wendell, *The Unsettling of America* (San Francisco: Sierra Club Books, 1977) p. 62.

Is Local Organic Food "Elitist"?

1   Center for Media and Democracy, Sourcewatch, www.sourcewatch.org/index.php/Center_for_Consumer_Freedom#Corporations.

2   Ness, Carol, "Hand that feed bites back: Food industry forks over ad campaign to win hearts, stomachs", *San Francisco Chronicle*, May 11, 2002.

3   https://www.consumerfreedom.com/about/.

4   Brandon, Hembree, "Environmental elites overlook human needs", *American Agriculturist*, January 3, 2003.

5   "Organic diet called 'elitist and arrogant'", *Salt Lake City Desert News*, April 29, 2001, cited in Centre for Safe Food at the University of Guelph, http://archives.foodsafetynetwork.ca/agnet/2001/5-2001/ag-05-01-01-02.txt.

Young Farmers in Ladakh

1   The film can be viewed at https://vimeo.com/528963024.

The Sharing Economy: It Takes More than a Smartphone

1   Yan, Yunxiang, "Gifts", Cambridge Encyclopedia of Anthropology, July 7, 2020. https://www.anthroencyclopedia.com/entry/gifts.

2   Botsman, Rachel, "The case for collaborative consumption", TED.com, presented at TEDxSydney, May 2010.

3   "Brands", Denimology.com; "Number of apps available in leading app stores in 2022/2023", Finances Online.

4   According to the "Chief Sharer" for the web-based non-profit The People Who Share, the sharing economy encompasses "swapping, exchanging, collective purchasing, collaborative consumption, shared ownership,

shared value, co-operatives, co-creation, recycling, upcycling, re-distri-bution, trading used goods, renting, borrowing, lending, subscription based models, peer-to-peer, collaborative economy, circular economy, on-demand economy, gig economy, crowd economy, pay-as-you-use economy, wikinomics, peer-to-peer lending, micro financing, micro-en-trepreneurship, social media, the Mesh, social enterprise, futurology, crowdfunding, crowdsourcing, cradle-to-cradle, open source, open data, user generated content (UGC) and public services"—a definition so broad it is meaningless. Matofska, Benita, "What is the Sharing Econ-omy?" The People Who Share, Sept 1, 2016.

5   https://companiesmarketcap.com.

6   Kell, John, "Avis to Buy Car-Sharing Service Zipcar", *Wall Street Journal*, Jan 2, 2013.

7   Jardin, Xeni, "Former Uber engineer alleges sexist abuse in workplace, CEO Travis Kalanick responds", Boing Boing, Feb 19, 2017.

8   Slee, Tom, "The Sharing Economy's Dirty Laundry", *Jacobin* magazine, March 23, 2016.

9   "The Sharing Economy Consumer Views Survey", Veridu and The People Who Share, May 2016.

10   "Tool library", Wikipedia.

Small Loans, Big Problems:
The False Promise of Microfinance

1   Hickel, Jason, "The microfinance delusion: who really wins?", *The Guard-ian*, June 10, 2015.

2   Grandolini, Gloria, "Helping the world's one billion unbanked women", *The Guardian*, June 11, 2015. Paid content sponsored by VISA.

3   Richey, Ellen, and Hannig, Alfred, "Meeting of the minds: why policy makers and the private sector should work together on financial inclu-sion", *The Guardian*, April 13, 2015. Paid content sponsored by VISA.

Thinking Outside the Grid

1   https://www.50waystohelp.com/.

2   Although IBM's "Smarter Planet Initiative" has ended, an IBM history of the campaign is available on their website, https://www.ibm.com/ibm/history/ibm100/us/en/icons/smarterplanet/.

3   Lagos, Marisa, "Californians Are Angry at PG&E Over Blackouts", KQED (San Francisco), October 23, 2019.

Climate Solutions: Real and Not-so-Real

1   Plotnikova, Sasha, "Designing for a world after climate catastrophe", UnevenEarth.com, October 22, 2019.

ABOUT THE AUTHORS

BAYO AKOMOLAFE was born to Yoruba parents in western Nigeria, and now lives between India and the United States. He is a widely celebrated international speaker, teacher, public intellectual, and essayist, and is the author of two books, *These Wilds Beyond our Fences: Letters to My Daughter on Humanity's Search for Home* and *We Will Tell our Own Story: The Lions of Africa Speak.* He has taught at Middlebury College, Sonoma State University, Simon Fraser University, and Schumacher College, and currently lectures at Pacifica Graduate Institute and the University of Vermont. In 2021 he was the recipient of the New Thought Walden Award.

HENRY COLEMAN connected with the work of Local Futures at age 15, and has worked with the organization in Ladakh, India and Australia since 2015. Now almost fluent in Ladakhi, he helps to coordinate Local Futures' projects there, and also represents Local Futures through his writing and at public events. In 2017, he co-founded the NGO Wildspace, where he has further developed his capacity as a community organizer and activist.

KUNZANG DEACHEN is the Project Associate/Coordinator for Local Futures Ladakh, and actively collaborates with local NGOs. Among the many projects she has contributed to are a book of folk songs about mountains, glaciers and rivers called *Singing Ice,* and a campaign stressing the importance of the *goba* (traditional governance) system in Ladakh.

STEVEN GORELICK has worked with Local Futures since 1987. He is the co-director of the film *The Economics of Happiness,* author of *Small is Beautiful, Big is Subsidized,* and co-author of *Bringing the Food Economy Home.* He is editor-in-chief for Local Futures, and has been published on Resilience, Counterpunch and numerous other online publications, and in *The Ecologist* and *Resurgence* magazines. He and his spouse run a small-scale organic farm in Vermont.

ALEX JENSEN has worked with Local Futures in the USA and India, where he coordinates the organization's Ladakh Project. He has worked at the Sambhaavnaa Institute of Public Policy and Politics in Himachal Pradesh, India, and represents Local Futures in the Vikalp Sangam/ Alternatives India initiative. He has worked with cultural affirmation and agro-biodiversity projects in campesino communities in a number of countries, and is active in environmental health/anti-toxics work.

MARJANA KOS has worked with Local Futures since 2006. She holds a Master's degree in Holistic Science from Schumacher College, and is active in raising awareness about globalization, new economics, the money system and complementary currencies in her native Slovenia. With her partner and young son, she is creating a one-hectare forest garden and building a low-impact, natural home.

ANJA LYNGBAEK has worked with Local Futures since 1986 on many projects, including the International Alliance for Localization, the Economics of Happiness Conference Series, and World Localization Day. Fluent in Spanish, English and Danish, she has been a spokesperson for localization on several continents. Anja divides her time between a Mexican ecovillage and a small island in the Danish Archipelago. She is a passionate food grower and is happiest with her hands in the soil. She holds a BSc in Rural Resource Management and a MPhil. in Agroforestry.

HELENA NORBERG-HODGE is the founder and director of Local Futures, and the convenor of World Localization Day. She is author of *Local is Our Future* and the inspirational classic *Ancient Futures*, and producer of the award-winning documentary The Economics of Happiness.A pioneer of the new economy movement, she founded the International Alliance for Localization, and co-founded the International Forum on Globalization and the Global Ecovillage Network. She is a recipient of the Alternative Nobel prize, the Arthur Morgan Award and the Goi Peace Prize for contributing to "the revitalization of cultural and biological diversity, and the strengthening of local communities and economies worldwide."

CHOZIN PALMO is from the Changthang region of Ladakh. She is founder of the Jangsa initiative and co-organized the Ladakh Economics of Happiness conference. With Local Futures she is helping to raise awareness of the systemic roots of contemporary ecological, cultural and social issues in Ladakh, and to strengthen the local agrarian economy.

JIGMET SINGGE is from Chemday village, Ladakh, and has worked with Local Futures Ladakh since 2019. He is an outdoor enthusiast who is keen to connect with different people from Ladakh and the world. Singge is also a vocalist, farmer, student and professional worker.

KRISTEN STEELE has worked with Local Futures since 2000 in multiple roles, including research, writing, fundraising, outreach and program management. She has also been the main organizer for several Economics of Happiness conferences and other Local Futures' events. She holds a BA in Environmental Studies and a Master's degree in Wild Animal Biology. She is also currently pursuing doctoral research on the intersection of conservation and economics in regards to threatened species.

ABOUT LOCAL FUTURES

Local Futures works to renew ecological, social and spiritual well-being by promoting a systemic shift towards economic localization. An internationally respected advocate for new economies, Local Futures has been raising awareness about this issue for more than four decades.

Through our "education for activism" programs, we provide communities with a range of educational and practical tools for shifting direction—away from dependence on global monopolies, and towards decentralized, regional economies. Our award-winning film *The Economics of Happiness* (2011) is a central part of this work, and continues to be screened regularly throughout the world. Since 2020, we have convened an annual World Localization Day, partnering with hundreds of dedicated individuals and grassroots organizations around the world to celebrate and raise the visibility of the global movement for local economies. We also organize conferences under the Economics of Happiness banner, providing an international forum for localization advocates from diverse parts of the world to connect with each other.

Local Futures began as the Ladakh Project in 1978, and initially focused on supporting Ladakh's indigenous culture by exposing the idealized images of Western consumer culture that were flooding into the region through tourism and development. Together with Ladakhi leaders, Local Futures established the first NGOs in the region, promoted organic agriculture, and developed a range of renewable energy technologies.

Since then, Local Futures has undertaken and supported numerous grassroots initiatives in both the global North and South. As a "think-and-do tank", we produce books, films, online materials, action guides, and even comic books aimed at strengthening ecological and social well-being, and we organize conferences, workshops, webinars and public lectures to disseminate the global-to-local perspective. One of the first NGOs worldwide to promote local food, Local Futures is still almost unique in doing so from an international perspective. We have produced several books and numerous reports critiquing industrial food and promoting local alternatives, and our multi-media *Local Food Tool-*

kit won the Derek Cooper Award for Investigative Journalism.

Today, Local Futures operates from offices in the US, UK, Mexico and Australia, with "sister" organizations in Germany and Japan.

To learn more about Local Futures' work, please go to www.localfutures.org, or contact us at info@localfutures.org.

LOCAL FUTURES
www.localfutures.org